LEE COUNTY LIBRARY
SANFORD, N. C.

WINNERS OF THE WEST

BY THE SAME AUTHOR

Bound and Gagged
Clown Princes and Court Jesters (with Samuel Gill)
Continued Next Week
World of Laughter
Kops and Custards (with Terry Brewer)
Collecting Classic Films

★★★

Winners of the West:
The Sagebrush Heroes of the Silent Screen

by
KALTON C. LAHUE

South Brunswick and New York: A. S. BARNES AND COMPANY
London: THOMAS YOSELOFF LTD

★★★

©1970 by A. S. Barnes and Co., Inc.
Library of Congress Catalogue Card Number: 72-107120

A. S. Barnes and Co., Inc.
Cranbury, New Jersey 08512

Thomas Yoseloff Ltd
108 New Bond Street
London W1Y OQX, England

ISBN 0-498-07396-3
Printed in the United States of America

Contents

Foreword		Fred Humes	186
Acknowledgements		Al Jennings	192
Art Acord	15	Buck Jones	199
Broncho Billy Anderson	25	J. Warren Kerrigan	209
Buzz Barton	31	Leo Maloney	216
Yakima Canutt	36	Ken Maynard	222
Harry Carey	43	Tim McCoy	232
Edmund Cobb	53	Tom Mix	241
Bill Coby	59	Pete Morrison	252
Lester Cuneo	69	Jack Perrin	259
Bob Custer	77	Buddy Roosevelt	267
William Desmond	87	Bob Steele	277
William Duncan	98	Roy Stewart	284
Franklyn Farnum	111	Fred Thomson	294
Hoot Gibson	120	Tom Tyler	304
Texas Guinan	129	Wally Wales	312
Neal Hart	138	Ted Wells	322
William S. Hart	148	Guinn "Big Boy" Williams	328
Helen Holmes	159	Jay Wilsey	333
Al Hoxie	167	And Others	341
Jack Hoxie	175		

To BETTY BURBRIDGE—For the countless hours of enjoyment and thrills which filled a childhood treasured through the years.

And my wife JULIE—For the most wonderful eight years of my life, and a devotion far beyond the call of connubial duty, without which this nor any other of my books could have been done.

Foreword

The reader is quite likely to disagree, perhaps violently, with some of the opinions and observations expressed on the following pages, so beware—this is a personal and quite subjective account of the life and death of the silent western and its heroes. It was undertaken with some apprehension, since I had retained fond memories from childhood of the late silent and early sound westerns, and having had the illusion of the Keystone legend shattered while researching *Kops and Custards* some years ago, I hesitated to search out the remaining silent westerns for review now, since it meant exposing the dark warmth of long-held recollections to the cold light of a more mature reality in a day and age much different from when they were formed.

Together with my wife Julie, who served as research assistant for this project, I spent virtually every night for over two months screening silent westerns—once the world's champion western fan, Harold Kinkade Jr., finally convinced me the book should be done. It was not so earth-shattering an experience as I had expected, but certain memories were found to be vague and many impressions were altered as a result. As film after film unreeled before our eyes, we arrived at several conclusions:

(1) While the western format was probably the most popular of all, a high percentage of the films available today, including those found only in very private collections, could only be described as bad.

(2) The repetition in plotting and story structure was unbelievable, a discovery which amused Arthur Henry Gooden, Betty Burbridge and other scriptwriters to whom we mentioned the fact. So little variation existed in the average western that stock numbers might easily be given as sufficient for plot description.

(3) Even viewed in the context of the era in which they were produced (as much as possible), the silent westerns lacked the very evil that eventually brought their demise—sound. As a format, the western was essentially an outdoors drama striving to recreate a reality it couldn't hope to convincingly reproduce without sound.

(4) The films themselves were not nearly so fascinating as the

people involved. And so we decided that it was not the western as a genre which needed illumination (Fenin and Everson had already done a most commendable job of that in their volume, *The Western, From Silents to Cinerama*), it was the western star whose return from the obscurity of time would prove most interesting to the reader.

As a result, you will find the book organized in sections, each representing a genuine western star or personality. No actors who merely interpreted the West, as George O'Brien or the Farnum brothers, are included. Many of the contenders from which the ultimate choice was made are not represented at all, or just mentioned briefly in passing, but as some boundaries had to be established we picked those who seemed to be most representative of the silent sagebrush heroes, a choice with which you may disagree.

Acknowledgments

The number of contributors to this volume makes it possible to name only a few and my many thanks go to each and every western fan who wrote, telephoned or appeared in person once word of this endeavor reached them. But special thanks have to be given to certain individuals for their outstanding efforts, and so to Harold Kinkade Jr. and Anthony Phillips goes credit for the book's concept; to Robert Cotten and Frank Pascoe, profuse appreciation for their deep interest in Tim McCoy and Lester Cuneo, which helped shape those sections of the book; to Winfred J. Horwood, Francis P. Clark, Cyril Nicholls, Nick Fiorentino, Robert and Charles Smith, Robert Pillows, the National Film Archive, London and others, my gratitude for the use of stills and films; to the many individuals behind the scene, of whom Richard Thorpe, George Marshall, Ray Ries, Arthur Henry Gooden, Louise Lorraine and Ed Cobb are but a few, my sincere thanks, and to the gentleman who prefers anonymity to surround his collection of Lester Scott's Action Pictures, my thanks for lifting the curtain of time briefly.

Art Acord

Art Acord—the mention of his name is sufficient to open wide the flood gate of memories for those who recall him, or to bring forth but a vacant stare from those who were not among the legion of fans who admired the screen exploits of this tall, melancholy stranger. An expert horseman, fighter and all-around cowpuncher, Acord found himself in the unusual position of being loved by those fans who identified with him or completely ignored by those who did not—a most peculiar circumstance for a screen hero, but one which he helped to create.

A genuine cowboy from Stillwater, Oklahoma Territory, and the last of 11 children, Art was an orphan almost from birth. It was a lonely childhood and those who knew him best swear that the sadness which characterized his features had been permanently etched during his youth. Of the many ways to make a living young Acord tried, Art chose to become a rodeo rider. His specialty was winning championships and he was rather good at it. Lured to the movies in 1911 by their incredible demand for stunt riders and the easy money involved, Acord existed as best he could, periodically returning to the rodeo circuits, as in 1912 when he carried away the world's championship in steer bulldogging at Pendleton, Oregon, by setting a steer-throwing record of 24 seconds. Four years later, he would duplicate the feat at New York's famed "Stampede" in competition against his best friend, Hoot Gibson.

In 1915, Art was cast as the lead in American's adaptation of Charles Van Loan's "Buck Parvin" stories. A perfect replica of the hero that Van Loan had created for his popular *Saturday Evening Post* series, Acord struck a responsive chord, and for the first time in years began to reap the long-delayed adulation which feeds a screen actor's ego. But just as his starring career moved into gear, America entered World War I and Art left the screen to defend the colors. Sent to France with the Fourth Division, Acord won the Croix-de-Guerre at Verdun, returning home an authentic hero in 1919.

Art Acord.

Unlike many, Art did not have to start at the bottom again when he reappeared in Hollywood after being discharged. He was signed to a three-year contract to make western short subjects and serials for Universal. One of his first to hit the screen was *The Moon Riders,* an 18-episode chapter play die-hard Acord fans have never forgotten. Giving Art his first taste of real stardom, *The Moon*

An early Selig western (circa 1910) with Eugenie Besserer, Tom Santschi, Herbert Rawlinson, Art Acord, Hobart Bosworth, Iva Shepard and "Daddy" Richardson.

Riders proved to be extremely popular in 1920 and still remains high on the list of lost but desirable collectors' items.

Caught off-guard by this box-office success, Universal had no follow-up script ready and while waiting for Ford I. Beebe to script a western tale of the supernatural, Art, his wife Edythe Sterling and Pete Morrison made 5 two-reelers for Dominant Pictures Corporation in late 1920. As soon as Beebe had his script underway, Universal rushed Acord into *The White Horseman*, which ultimately proved to be almost as popular as *The Moon Riders* and assured Art a permanent place as one of the movies' foremost exponents of the western genre. But at this point, the new star's career reached a plateau and even though he continued making features and serials until just before his death in 1931, Acord never became a stellar attraction on the order of Hoot Gibson or Buck Jones.

His failure to achieve more had nothing to do with talent; as western stars went, Art Acord had many assets and was ruggedly handsome in the sort of way that made women want to mother him. But there was one liability. Art possessed a weakness which he was unable to overcome—his Achilles heel was in the shape of a bottle. While his contemporaries—cowpunchers, rodeo riders and

Art Acord, Mildred Moore and Tote DuCrow in The Moon Riders, *Art's legendary Universal serial of 1920.*

other western stars like Jack Hoxie and Hoot Gibson—all had a fondness for hard liquor and a rousing good time, they were able to control the temptation; Acord simply couldn't. During a severe bout, the actor would disappear for days, even weeks at a time, and when he returned it was with the firm resolve never to touch the stuff again. After an especially hard drinking session, Art would refuse to answer his telephone for weeks at a time, literally breaking into a cold sweat and nervous twitch whenever it rang. It was not without justification that Art feared "sociable" calls from his friends; his circle of drinking companions refused to take him seriously and would badger Acord until he broke down.

The Acord westerns usually found him cast as the wandering stranger; wherever Art's screen character went, it was in the guise of the mysterious vagabond, often running from the law (either justifiably or not) but one who rode into situations not of his own making and whose remorse for his past brought forth a feeling of responsibility to give others his help. This theme of self-sacrifice was one to which he was perfectly mated and it appeared time and time again in films like *Loco Luck, Sky High Corral, The White Outlaw* and *The Arizona Kid.* His talent was undeniable, not as an actor per se, but as a screen personality and although many of his later pictures turned out to be potboilers, brief flashes of his potential could be seen even as late as 1928.

Art's alcoholism was an illness for which there was no physical cure; he was a very sick man and by the mid-twenties had reached the stage where even the odor of liquor acted as a trigger. Unfortunately, the only answer for Acord's problem was will power, the one thing he was unable to muster in sufficient quantity to help himself. When his contract expired in 1923, Universal was only too happy to see him leave. He managed to make a triumphant tour of South America with a western show troupe in 1924, and while making a series for Truart Pictures managed to convince Universal that he was a changed man. But it soon became apparent that he was the same Art Acord who had previously caused Universal's production schedules so much grief.

While other western stars turned out eight or more features a season with ease, Acord had great difficulty in making the usual eight. The resulting films were spasmodic in release and uneven in quality, and Art was forced to finish out his career working for Exhibitors' Film Corporation and other independents who could

Acord runs the Indian gauntlet In The Days of Buffalo Bill.

Among his other problems In The Days of Buffalo Bill, *Art had to reckon with the perfidy of the villainous Indian chief.*

dash off a completed picture during his increasingly infrequent sober periods.

Like most hard drinkers, Art Acord was a totally different person once under the influence; his extremely likeable and gentle nature would become belligerent hostility. His slender physical appearance belied a tremendous strength—he was noted for the ability to drive his fist through a barroom wall unharmed—and Acord spent as much time recovering from the effects of barroom brawls as he did from the barroom itself. But the agonizing slavery

Dr. Marcus Whitman's journey along The Oregon Trail *to carry the word of God to the Northwest Indians depended upon Art, who also fought a vicious fur syndicate in his spare time.*

Loco Luck, *1926.*

Art Acord, Louise Lorraine (his wife in real life) and ZaZu Pitts.

to a cruel master was to end shortly; talkies were bringing a whole new discipline to the screen.

Contrary to the popular legend that has been perpetuated by writers who have dealt with the western, Acord's rich, mellow voice would have been perfectly suited to the medium of sound, had he been able to learn and deliver his lines without difficulty; two of his former wives who worked steadily in talkies agreed on this point. But few producers were willing to invest their money trying to disprove his long-established and well-founded reputation, and so a despondent and sick man who could find no peace of mind

Toward the end of his career, Art put on considerable weight, losing the fine features he had once possessed. In 1931, he would die in Mexico under mysterious circumstances.

*One of Art's last roles was the sentimental tale of a bandit who sacrificed himself to save his friend—*The White Outlaw.

in his search for sobriety went south of the border with a western act. He never returned.

While his death on January 4, 1931, in Mexico was reported two days later by the Mexican authorities as resulting from alcohol poisoning, reports circulated that his body contained enough cyanide to kill several men, and close friends still claim that he was knifed as the result of a barroom brawl and that his obituary as reported in the American press was an effort to avoid an international incident at a time when the United States and Mexico were attempting to work out political difficulties without emotionalism. And so Art Acord passed into the sunset of memory. Regrettably, too few of his films are available for viewing today; had he been able to conquer his all-consuming thirst, there is little reason to doubt that this unhappy cowpoke would most certainly rank today as one of the silent screen's leading western heroes—but not all of life's stories have a happy ending.

Broncho Billy Anderson

While somewhat ironic, it was also quite in keeping with the world of make-believe that the first western screen hero couldn't ride a horse, had never been West of Chicago and bore the unlikely name of Max Aronson. In spite of these shortcomings, which one would imagine to be handicaps to any enterprising would-be actor, G. M. Anderson, as he was known, saw opportunity knock and lassoed it with a dexterity that would have made any cowpoke of the old West hold his breath. From a chance role in Edwin Porter's *The Great Train Robbery* in 1903, Anderson rose to prominence as "Broncho Billy" and half-owner of one of the most respected of the pioneer production firms, Essanay. It all came to pass because of blind luck, sheer desperation and a goodly portion of faith.

Cast in Porter's film as one of the bandits on his assurance that he could ride like a Texas Ranger, Anderson promptly fell off his horse and was recast as an extra. Undaunted by this demotion, Anderson saw a future in movies and landed a job at Vitagraph. By 1907, he had moved to Chicago, where he took a Selig unit to Colorado to make a number of westerns—films that both audiences and Selig failed to properly appreciate. Leaving the indifferent producer, Anderson looked up George K. Spoor, an old friend, and together they founded Essanay, with headquarters in Chicago.

But Anderson still felt the western film was destined to become the most popular genre of this new entertainment medium, and in the fall of 1908 he appeared in Niles, California, to establish a West Coast studio for Essanay. Thinking back on his experiences at Selig, he decided that his error had been one of trying to follow the formula of Porter's film too closely. What was needed, Anderson sensed, was a central character with whom the audience could identify. The logical move was to create a cowboy hero, the precursor of hundreds who would ride among the celluloid sagebrush over the next two decades. Unable to find an actor in the wilds of central California who was willing to risk his professional career in such a venture, the desperate producer had no choice but to undertake

the chore himself. And so G. M. Anderson became producer, director and actor. But stuntman he was not, and this first of the western stars was also the first to make regular use of a double in his films. Reputedly taking his screen name from a Peter B. Kyne story, "Broncho Billy and the Baby," Anderson's first Broncho Billy western was *Broncho Billy's Redemption*, released on July 30, 1910.

Broncho Billy was no actor, as his early films bear out. But he had been correct in his estimation of the audiences and the popularity of his films was unmatched by anything the competition had to offer. Heavy-set and solidly built, with no fluidity or grace in his movements, Anderson was past the bloom of youth and could not, by any stretch of the imagination, be considered a handsome hero; but his appearance was striking, accentuated by a cold glint in his eyes that made audiences believe this *was* a man of the West. For the next six years, Anderson appeared as Broncho Billy in a single reel western almost weekly, in addition to numerous appearances in straight dramatic roles outside the western character.

Critics and historians have tended to depreciate the Broncho Billy films as portraying a "dime novel" West that never existed. But as more and more of his short westerns have been retrieved from the murky pages of history, it becomes quite clear to the viewer that they did possess a starkly documentary quality which reflected the West later seen by William S. Hart. As with the majority of Essanay films of the period, the Broncho Billy westerns were characterized by sharp photography and the excellent camera work of Rollie Totheroh, who later served as Charlie Chaplin's cameraman for over 30 years. The western sets were elaborate and realistic in appearance far beyond what was usually found in films of the time, all of which added up to solid production values in support of the star.

Of course, with the great demands made by the necessity of a new reel of film each week, little thought was given at first to any consistency of character in this first of the western series and Broncho Billy could be seen as a lawman one week and a die-hard villain the next. He was even killed off at the end of several films, only to return the following week. But before long, this inconsistency came to Anderson's attention and his response was a combination of the two, pioneering the concept of the "good/bad man," which later proved to be Bill Hart's springboard to success. Broncho Billy's single reels did not possess the story qualities that characterizes the

Broncho Billy's Adventure, *1911.*

Anderson pioneered the "good-badman" characterization later perfected by William S. Hart. This scene is from "Broncho Billy and The Maid".

Hart westerns, but in the six years he appeared on-screen in Broncho Billy's garb, Anderson bridged the path from simple to complex stories in a single reel. For the time in which they were made, films such as *Broncho Billy's Sentence* (a February 1915 release) are amazing for the degree of complexity involved, and there was not

The Bearded Bandit, *1912*.

a single foot of film which failed to advance the plot in a logical but rapid manner. Opening with Broncho Billy as a bandit attempting to elude capture by a posse, the central theme revolved around his conversion to the side of law and order by the kind treatment given him at the hands of a minister. His reformation by the minister and the Bible involved several scenes of reflective contemplation leading to character alterations unquestionably superior in a film of this kind.

But by 1916, Broncho Billy was feeling the winds of change that were sweeping the movie industry. The feature picture of five reels or more was consolidating its dominance over the shorter subjects. General Film, which released Essanay's films, was no longer competitive with Mutual, Universal and the other distributors. George K. Spoor opposed the investment necessary to produce features and G. M. Anderson was tired. Selling his half of Essanay, the actor-director-executive retired Broncho Billy to become an independent producer. Never again would he know the fame or financial security which Broncho Billy had brought. Retiring from the industry altogether in 1923, G. M. Anderson came back to the screen in 1965 with a cameo role in Alex Gordon's *The Bounty Hunters*, capping a

A stern warning to Brinsley Shaw from Sheriff Bill. Broncho Billy and the Rustler's Child, *1913.*

career that had carried him from obscurity into the hearts of millions as Broncho Billy, the first of the western screen idols.

Buzz Barton

The year 1927 was an epochal one in several respects—Babe Ruth hit 60 home runs, setting a new major league record; Charles Lindbergh flew the Atlantic in the tiny *Spirit of St. Louis* and the silent western entered a decline from which it could not recover. The large influx of independent producers after World War I had made the industry's release schedule topheavy with oaters during the twenties and while two top stars (Ken Maynard and Fred Thomson) emerged from their ranks, the majority of western stars were virtually finished as leading men by 1930.

The arrival of some—like Ted Wells, Fred Humes and Buzz Barton—came too late in the twenties for them to gain a firm following before sound swept their fragile starring careers away. Of these, probably 12-year-old Barton stood the best chance of survival, but even the most talented western performers found the late twenties rough going. Buzz, whose real name was Billy Lamar, got his start in Jack Perrin's Rayart westerns at the age of 11, and with his red hair and profuse freckles he attracted considerable attention; he went directly from the Perrin westerns into his own starring series for FBO in 1927. Directed mainly by Louis King, these FBO films were tailor-made for the youthful hero and quite good as a result. An excellent horseman for his age, Barton was easily the equal of several stars who had ridden for years and the master of many others. Written mainly by Frank Howard Clark, his scripts incorporated this ability, as well as his talent with a rope, as the central focus of action.

The only real competition to Buzz came from Newton House, Universal's "Champion Boy Rider" who, although only a few years older, had already started to lose the boyish appeal Barton still retained. But even the youngster's appealing personality and his wizardry in the saddle were not sufficient to overcome a basic fact of life—for most audiences, the western had lost its fascination. This was caused in part by the reluctance of the major production companies to commit themselves to a genre whose once-golden box-

Buzz Barton.

office appeal had now begun to look like brass, and it was compounded by the fact that minor independent producers stepped in to fill the vacuum with a shoddy product that further alienated the fans. This void, which had developed in the market during 1928–29, was filled by the poorly-made films of Syndicate, Robert J. Horner, William Pizor, J. Charles Davis and others—films which stretched the credulity of fans, even the younger ones, to a breaking point and insulted the intelligence of mature audiences.

Cast under his real name in the Jack Perrin Rayart series, Billy Lamar was a hit. Billy, on the horse, listens to advice from Jack in **The Laffin' Fool.**

Figures tell the story most vividly: In 1925, the Motion Picture Theatre Owners Association commissioned a study of the most popular films exhibited by their members. Theatre owners were surveyed during the 1926–27 season and the final report contained a total of 208 features, the cream of the crop in terms of attendance. Of these, nearly 30 percent, or 60 films, had been westerns. In October 1929, *Film Daily* polled the top 10 production companies for a projected breakdown of their 1929–30 product. None reported a single western to be in the works at that time. Reaching deeper into the industry, the trade paper then polled a total of 45 producers, both major and independents. This produced a list of but 50 new westerns, 29 of which would contain sound in one form or another, and almost all of them were from the minor independents.

Even though Buzz Barton's films were well done, the sight of a teenager and his screen heroics was not calculated to resurrect the western from the grave others had prepared for it. As a tired format wheezed to its inevitable end, Buzz dropped from leading roles, to reappear in supporting parts in the multitude of independent talkies in the thirties, which arose phoenix-like from the ashes of the silent western. Like that of many child stars, Barton's lustre tarnished at an early age and he was never again to know the fame that greeted his work in 1926–29.

As Buzz Barton, Billy went into his own series for FBO. Here is The Little Buckaroo.

Barton's red hair and freckles added to his youthful charm.

In that awkward transitional period between silents and talkies, Buzz Barton suffered a decline in popularity. Here he is with Wally Wales in Big 4's 1931 Riders of The Cactus.

Buzz ended his career in independent westerns playing the sidekick to Rex Bell and other stars.

★★

Yakima Canutt

Probably the best known and most capable second-unit director in the business, Yakima Canutt has successfully pursued several careers in his 74 years—rodeo rider, movieland stunt double, action star in his own western series, supporting actor and master stunt stage. This is quite a series of accomplishments for any one person. Born Enos Edward Canutt, Yak acquired his unusual nickname through a misplaced picture caption and an erroneous introduction by an announcer at the Pendleton (Oregon) Roundup of 1914. It was great for the rodeo circuits, but something of a tongue-twister for his later matinee fans.

The rodeo led to Hollywood, where the increasing awareness of a star's value to his producer was rapidly expanding the profession of stuntman, and Canutt took particular pride in his ability to ride (and stay on) any horse alive. Yak stunted and played small parts for Universal and other studios until 1924, when Ben Wilson put him under contract for a series of western features which Arrow released (*Branded a Bandit, Ridin' Mad, Romance and Rustlers*) and this mile-a-minute star delivered the goods so well that Wilson was able to move his release to FBO (Film Booking Office) the following season. Better stories and production values resulted in a series that included *Scar Hanan, The Riding Comet, King of The Rodeo* and *White Thunder*. Yakima continued making independent westerns during the twenties, working for Goodwill (*Hell Hound of the Plains, The Iron Rider*), Bell Pictures (*Three Outcasts, Bad Men's Money*) and others, but for all of his talent, Canutt never made it into the winner's circle with his starring roles. Fame was not to come to Yakima Canutt for his exploits as a leading man.

Filled with fast-moving action and snappy stunt work guaranteed to raise the blood pressure of the most bored patron, Canutt's starring pictures were pure delight for the confirmed western adventure addict. Fans could usually count on this hero to come through in a big way and unusual opening sequences became something of a trademark; in *The Iron Rider*, Yakima's lady friend was awaiting

36

Yakima Canutt.

his arrival while fending off an over-amorous admirer, who also happened to have evil designs on both her and her property. The camera cut away from this scene to a long shot of the open plain near the hacienda—and sure enough, there was Canutt riding like the wind to her rescue—standing upright on his horse and waving his hat! Yakima's screen exploits on horseback were nearly the equal of Ken Maynard's (and a contest between these two would have been the show of the century), but while Ken's trick riding was written in as an integral part of his stories, Canutt's stunt riding was an overlay of pure showmanship.

A handsome devil who cut a striking figure on-screen, Yak had several strikes against him in a bid for screen stardom—release of his films by an independent (Arrow) whose access was mainly to the neighborhood theatres, an almost unpronounceable name and producers interested mainly in the fast dollar—all restricted his potential. Always in a light-hearted vein, his portrayals had an air of unreality about them and he no doubt suffered from audience disbelief that one man could perform so many varied and daring feats without the aid of doubles or camera tricks. While his stunting was far more breathtaking than that of Fred Thomson, Yakima was never able to win over the non-western fans and build his appeal across a broad base as did Thomson.

Canutt's most outstanding contributions to the screen came after he left starring roles and returned to supporting parts and stunting. While early stuntmen were simply more foolhardy (and less valuable) than the stars they replaced, Yakima was one of the new breed who carefully analyzed the risks involved and then figured every conceivable alternative—a process that helped to considerably extend

Canutt in the full western garb he wore in the twenties and early thirties.

Yak has a few choice words for lovable old Nelson McDowell in Goodwill's The Outlaw Breaker.

a stunt double's useful life. The tragic and useless death of daredevil Jean Perkins in 1923 while doubling in one of William Desmond's serials pointed up the wisdom of Yak's approach. His refusal to do a stunt did not mean that it was impossible, but simply that the odds against its successful completion were too great to make it worthwhile.

But Yakima Canutt also performed some stunts that looked easy on the screen, although many of these, like his driving a team of horses and buggy off a cliff in *Dark Command,* required split-second timing and judgment. By the early thirties, Yak had become the leading stuntman at Mascot, Monogram and several of the independent studios. While playing mostly villainous roles, Canutt doubled Harry Carey, Rex Bell, John Wayne, Roy Rogers and dozens of other stars over the next two decades, as well as anyone else in the cast who was required to fight or fall. As a leading executor of stunts, it was natural progression for Yak to graduate to the staging of stunt-action for other directors and then to his own second-unit work.

Beginning in the late twenties, Yak switched from starring roles to supporting parts, usually as the villain. Here he menaces Wally Wales, who is determined that not even Yak can stop him from Carrying The Mail.

The Fighting Stallion.

Yak's greatest contribution to the screen came in his action and stunting sequences. This leap from the wagon was one of his specialties and shot from a distance, allowed him to double virtually any star.

Greed of Gold.

Over the years, the sure hand of Yakima Canutt has put a variety of thrills on celluloid; the prairie fire scene from *Dakota*, the oil wagons escaping through a blazing canyon in *In Old Oklahoma*, the chase across the salt flats in *Stagecoach*, the jousting scenes in *Ivanhoe*, the chariot race of *Ben Hur* and the battle scenes in *El Cid* and *Khartoum*. But Yak is best remembered today by fans of the "B" western for his often-imitated speciality—the transfer from horseback to the rear of a speeding stagecoach and the difficult climb to its top to engage the villain in a life and death struggle, only to fall between the horses in momentary defeat. Hanging on for a few seconds, he will finally let go, and as the coach passes over him grab the rear axle; then, slowly turning over on his stomach, he will climb to the top of the coach again and finish off the fight for good. Once standard matinee fare, you don't see this type of bone-breaking action as often today; and when it is done, it's seldom done as smoothly as when Canutt was plying his trade.

Too old to carry on in this manner today, Yakima Canutt's glory is in the past but in the forties and fifties, he trained an entire corps of stunt men who have perpetuated variations of the many thrills Yak originally designed for the screen and no one more richly deserves the place of honor he occupies in our memories than this dean of the western stunt epics.

★★★

Harry Carey

(THE MAN OF THE WEST)

Interestingly enough, a majority of the silent western screen favorites were Eastern dudes, some of whom were barely able to perform the required feats of roping, riding and roughhousing. Of the city boys who went West, a few became better at portraying western heroics than the native sons, and as a result won fame and fortune far from the streets of Brooklyn and the Bronx. Harry Carey was one of these transplanted sagebrush heroes whose popularity and durability went unquestioned.

The son of a New York City judge, Carey studied law at both Hamilton Institute and New York University. Recovering from an attack of pneumonia in 1899, he wrote a play to pass time. Encouraged by friends, Harry produced and starred in his own play, which he had called *Montana,* touring the country for five years. Its success was followed by a second Carey effort, *The Heart of Alaska,* but this one proved to be a failure and, looking for work, Harry drifted into the movies.

Finding his way to Biograph, Harry Carey spent several years working under the direction of D. W. Griffith, playing western and non-western roles with equal skill. By the time he joined Universal in 1915, Carey was instantly recognizable on-screen but was far from a star. Nearly 40, his rugged features made him an ideal western hero, but he had acquired considerable finesse in his acting and Universal used him in society dramas before casting the taciturn actor in *A Knight of The Range.* Directed by John Ford, this 1915 western resulted in a large step toward stardom and introduced him to his future wife. Harry courted his 18-year old leading lady, Olive Golden Fuller, and married her five years later.

The Carey westerns were not unlike the Hart features; Harry was a dedicated actor whose individuality warmed the screen with its casual approach but his homespun humor contained a touch of Will Rogers and the resulting characterization stood out as unique

Harry Carey.

at a time when many western stars were but carbon copies of each other, with very little to raise any particular one above the crowd. Other than Hart, John Ford was one of the few directors to present his heroes as human, pulling an extra dimension from his actors regardless of the roles being played. Like Hart, Carey possessed a suitable Victorian streak in his treatment of women and the old-

Winifred Westover and Harry in Marked Men.

Molly Malone and Harry in The Phantom Riders.

Blue Streak McCoy *was typical of the rugged roles Harry played.*

fashioned virtues of home and hearth; in a sense he pre-dated Hart in this trait, as he was an accomplished screen actor years before Hart made his first film.

For the next eight years, Harry Carey appeared in dozens of western short subjects and features under the Universal banner; among them were strong and unusual films like *The Freeze-Out,* in which he played the stranger who came to a small western town and found the gambling house to be crooked. Planning to build and operate his own saloon, Harry was charmed by Helen Ferguson and when his saloon finally opened, it was as a library and school. His action converted the entire town to a God-fearing life. In a whimsical ending, which detracted from the reality inherent in most Carey westerns, the other saloon owner also reformed in the closing scenes and donated his business establishment for use as a church.

Leaving Universal in 1922, Harry filmed several westerns (*Crashing Through, The Kickback, Desert Driven*) for FBO release, and in 1924 he joined forces with independent producer Hunt Stromberg to star in two series of features which should have established him as the logical successor to William S. Hart. Directed by Lloyd Ingraham, Reeves Eason and Tom Forman, and utilizing the excellent camerawork of Sol Polito, the authentic stories of Carey's PDC series ranged across the breadth of the West. *Silent Sanderson* found him in the Yukon, while *The Badlands* essayed early California; *Texas Trail, The Flaming Forties, The Nighthawk* and *The Prairie Pirate* kept Harry on the move in strong westerns, which still hold up well even today. But PDC (Producers Distributing Corporation) did not have the distribution facilities of a Paramount or Universal, and although Carey's fans continued to enjoy his remarkably strong roles the PDC films did not bring Harry the recognition he deserved.

Somewhat discouraged with his failure to firmly nail down the elusive fame Hoot Gibson, Buck Jones and Tom Mix enjoyed, Harry left Stromberg in 1925. Reappearing on the screen in 1926 under the Pathé banner, Carey worked steadily in fine westerns like *Satan Town, Border Patrol, Drifting Through* and *Burning Bridges* until early 1928, when he finished filming the series for 1928–29 release. Pathé did not renew the contract, and while Carey appeared on the screen into mid-1929, he was actually "at liberty." Harry had no financial worries at the time; his lengthy career had brought him sufficient monetary rewards for him to enjoy a large and well-stocked ranch.

But restless with the inactivity, he worked up a vaudeville act with his wife and set out on a tour of the hinterlands. On the night of March 15, 1928, the San Franciquito Dam burst and his ranch

The Man From Red Gulch, *one of Harry Carey's PDC westerns.*

The Prairie Pirate *was one of Harry's most respected roles and strongly emphasized his respect for womanhood, a strong link to William S. Hart's screen character.*

Harry's keeping bad company in **The Seventh Bandit.**

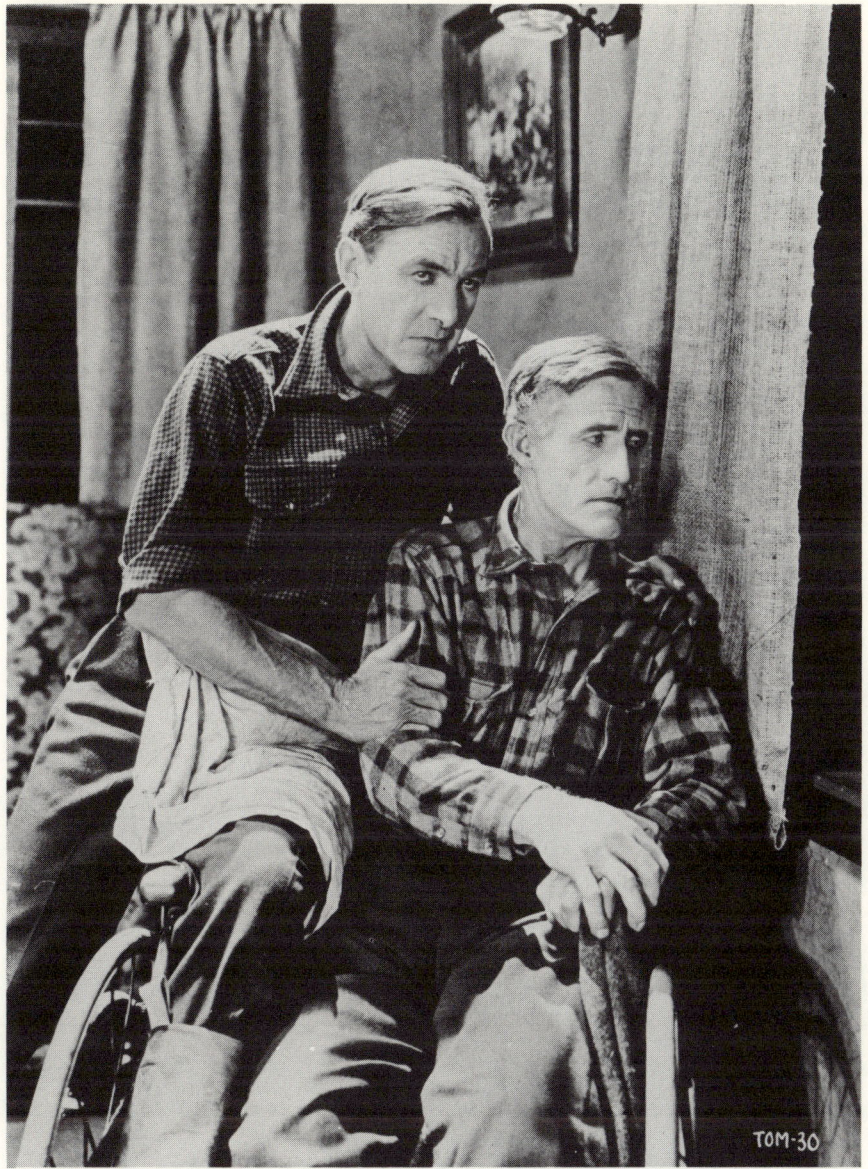

Crashin' Thru.

was directly in the path of the most damaging flood California had known in many years. As a result of the deluge 700 people lost their lives and Harry Carey was wiped out financially; he lost 750 sheep, 200 cattle and 60 horses.

Irving Thalberg came to the rescue, casting Harry in *Trader Horn*; and in March 1929, he left Culver City to spend the next seven months undergoing the hardships that plagued the location filming in Africa, but earning enough to rebuild and refurbish his

Harry protects Kathleen Collins in Pathé's Satan Town.

Harry Carey in one of his final silent roles, The Trail of '98.

In the mid-forties, Harry posed with a group of well-known western character actors from the silent days. Carey is standing at the center of the group, wearing the dark plaid shirt. The three riders directly behind him are Bill Gillis, Pedro Leon and Tommy Grimes. At the far right, Pedro Clemento stands undistinguishable beneath the sombrero. Directly in front of him is Joe Rickson, and to Joe's right, Neal Hart.

ranch. Hardly had he finished renovating the property when fire struck, and the entire ranch burned to the ground. Discouraged and dismayed, Harry worked hard to stay even, dividing his time between the stage, screen and circus tours. Carey managed a financial recovery but he was never able to regain the popularity he had enjoyed in the mid-twenties; younger actors had taken his place for good.

In his fifties now, Harry became a popular character actor, staying with the business until 1946 when a heart and lung condition forced his retirement. Bitten by a Black Widow spider at Balboa Beach in August 1947, Harry Carey died the following month of coronary thrombosis. His son, Harry DeWitt Carey III, carried on in westerns, billing himself first as Harry Carey Jr. and then simply Harry Carey, but never rose above the level of supporting actor.

Harry Carey was the last of his line. A new generation of moviegoers in the twenties had no conception of the real West, its virtues and vices. Accustomed to the action adventure epics, which had gradually replaced the realism engendered by Hart and Carey, their applause went to the younger western actors. But few who have seen or remember Harry Carey in any of his better silent westerns are likely to question his claim to the billing, "The Man of The West."

Edmund Cobb

No matter how bad the silent program westerns were, they had their followers in large numbers, and actors who otherwise would have found the practice of their chosen profession to be difficult if not impossible rose from the ranks of wranglers, stunt doubles and extras to a position of some prominence as leading men. Except for a brief period in the early to mid-thirties, such rewards for so little talent would not again come so easily in the celluloid world of the West until the advent of television. Some of the actors who specialized in western roles during the twenties would become well-known character actors of the sound era, and whatever reputation they enjoy with the public can be attributed specifically to that latter period in their careers.

Take Edmund Cobb, for example: A good-looking chap who rode a horse satisfactorily, handled a gun with sufficient skill and possessed the other minimum requirements for heroic roles, Ed Cobb had only one fault, which was apparent during most of his career in the silents—he couldn't act. One of the most unconvincing heroes of the silent screen, Ed found his niche as a character actor in the talkies, enjoying a favored position in the ranks of those who essayed the semi-heroics of supporting roles. Although in his later years Cobb seems to have appeared more often as a heavy, he was also quite often seen as the weak-kneed sheriff or cautious rancher who wanted no trouble with the world, and his work in these roles far outweighed the importance of his entire earlier career.

Ed was an Albuquerque, New Mexico, boy whose first screen work was done right in his home town for the St. Louis Motion Picture Company, which was there on location during 1910. At this early stage in the movies' development, leading men were somewhat difficult to come by, especially those possessing the talents needed for western heroics, and as a result, Ed enjoyed a slight reputation; at least he was available. By 1913, he was working for Lubin and the Romaine Fielding company shooting westerns in Las Vegas, New Mexico. When work with Fielding ran its course, Ed moved

Ed and Grace Cunard.

to the Canon City-Colorado Springs area where he free-lanced with the various companies filming in the vicinity throughout 1914. The next year, Cobb decided to try the big city and joined Essanay in Chicago.

Ed's career for the next few years was a study in obscurity; he played leading and secondary roles for a variety of companies but always in unimportant films; and as a result he managed to elude the multitude of producers looking for "promotable bodies" who could be press-agented into the "stardom" of independent films. But exhibitor demand for product continued and Ed surfaced in the early twenties under contract to Ben Wilson, a long-time screen actor whose major claim to fame was shared by Neva Gerber in the several chapter plays they had made together during 1917–21. Wilson then turned to production and direction for independent release, and for a few years in the twenties he had a flourishing business operating through Arrow release.

Too busy to personally supervise everything going on under his auspices, Wilson turned Ed over to Ashton Dearholt, another sometime actor-director and one at whom associates marveled for his success was founded (as they saw it) upon an almost total lack of

Ed starred in many of Universal's short westerns. Here he's about to put Paul C. Hurst in his place.

Alex Hart, Bill Cody, Ed and Richard Cummings in Cody's starring feature of 1926, The Galloping Cowboy.

knowledge about what he was doing. Within this framework, Ed made several features in 1922–23 (*At Devil's Gorge, Battling Bates, Sting of the Scorpion*) under Dearholt's supervision and another series in 1924 (*Western Feuds, Blasted Hopes*) under veteran Francis Ford's direction. None of these films received very good reviews and none are available today, but one of the worst serials to come out of this period, *Days of '49,* has survived and everything about it was pretty atrocious, including Ed Cobb and the fair Miss Gerber. If this was representative of Ed's feature work (and it seems to be—reviews of this chapter play, and the five-reel feature cut from it, were in the same vein as those of his features), it is unfair to place the blame entirely upon Cobb's shoulders; it rests mainly with Ben Wilson's poor direction and otherwise shoddy production.

I said earlier that Ed Cobb couldn't act—that was not quite truthful. The quality of his screen work was heavily dependent upon what he had to work with. Ed did some solid villainous portrayals in Bill Cody's pictures and a reasonably good job supporting Tim McCoy in *The Indians Are Coming,* the last of the silent serials, but he had well-written, carefully defined characterizations to fill. The Arrow westerns were haphazard affairs and did little to enhance his reputation in any direction.

Toward the end of his career in silent pictures, Ed undertook the role of a villain in addition to his heroic leads. Bill Cody warns him to leave Florence Uhlrich alone in The Galloping Cowboy.

Ed spent much of the twenties starring in the two-reel western shorts favored by Universal (*Hearts of The West, The Winged Rider, The Bashful Whirlwind*) and here again his work was erratic; some were good, most were not. The two-reelers were formula pictures, dashed off as Arthur Henry Gooden described them, "without much foresight or effort." Too short to allow the development of a distinctive characterization and personality, these short subjects were used by the neighborhood houses and were turned out on an assembly-line basis with the result that all looked alike. Forced to do his own stunts while at Arrow because of limited budgets, Ed was given the luxury of a stuntman in the Universal western shorts but the deception was made painfully evident by the somewhat primitive techniques of production used. An action sequence requiring a stunt double was filmed in medium shots until the climactic point, at which time the camera pulled way back for a long shot held until Ed's face had to be seen at the end of the hazardous action, then it cut back to a medium or close shot. Even the kids couldn't be fooled by that one and a star whose doubling was that apparent didn't rate very high with the small fry, especially if he were as romantically inclined as was Ed Cobb. Mushy love scenes were as much a drag to the young fans of silent westerns as were the cowboys who sang to their horses in the talkies.

Ed's none-too-spectacular career in the silents closed with his portrayal in *The Indians Are Coming,* the Universal serial that marked the end of silent serials and the opening of a new epoch in cliff-hanger history, the all-talking chapter play. This particular role has brought Ed a great deal of satisfaction over the years. He appeared at the beginning of the serial era in 1913's *The Adventures of Kathlyn* and presided over its demise in the role of Bill Williams, sidekick to Tim McCoy, in 1930.

His work in lesser roles continued through 1965 and Alex Gordon's Embassy release, *Requiem For A Gunfighter,* in which he rounded out a career that carried him over a half-century along the road of life and into the hearts of "B" western fans of the forties. You couldn't meet a nicer, unassuming cowpoke if you tried; retired at the time of this writing and living in North Hollywood, Ed Cobb occasionally pauses to wonder—what would it all have been like had he hit the top in a big way?

★★

Bill Cody

While many of the independent westerns of the twenties were inexcusably cheap exploitation pictures, designed to wring a fast quarter from the tightly clenched fists of the small fry who made up the Saturday matinee audience, the Bill Cody westerns stand out today as excellent examples of what could be done with a bit of money and talent, even on Poverty Row. Cody came to the movies with the usual stock and vaudeville background, none of which was particularly outstanding, and spent a number of years in the quiet obscurity which surrounded stuntmen—the real heroes of the horse operas. Although 33 when his first starring series began, Bill Cody still possessed the acrobatic finesse, superb physical condition and cat-like agility that had put him in great demand during the early twenties as a double for almost every western leading man in the business.

Jesse Goldburg's Independent Pictures Corporation signed Cody in 1924 for a group of five-reel westerns for state-right distribution, setting Bill on a starring career which he rode into the early days of sound pictures. The production values of his IPC pictures were outstanding for independent westerns—smooth and picturesque camerawork backed up by good scripting and an above-average supporting cast. As his feminine lead, Peggy O'Dare proved almost as daring as Bill, a refreshing change from the heroines who simply stood around and tried to look helpless. Cody's stories were plain, old-fashioned melodramas of the West, unrelieved by the comic influence which had all but overwhelmed some of the celluloid cowpokes of the period. They journeyed down well-traveled trails, capped by a conventional climax to be sure, but many thrills were encountered along the way.

Cody was a first-rate scrapper, and his films made good use of his fighting ability; unlike many of the staged fisticuffs, which were blatantly artificial and caused schoolboys to wonder where their hero (and the villain as well) had learned the manly art of self-defense, Bill's fight sequences were knock-down, drag-out brawls. In

Bill Cody.

contrast to other sagebrushers, Cody was not the superhuman hero who never lost a fight or his hat; he was properly whipped in film after film, but with a difference—he intentionally chose the largest, toughest and meanest-looking actors IPC casting could furnish for his opponents. In this way, Bill cleverly established a rapport with his audiences; when the slightly-built hero finally bested the towering villains in the final reel, it was an example of what clean living could do for anyone who refused to be tempted by tobacco, liquor and women—three vices he steered clear of on-screen.

Bill is all wrapped up in an exciting moment from **Border Justice.**

J. P. McGowan directed the IPC Cody series with a sure touch born of experience. One of the most versatile and prolific action directors in the business, McGowan wrote scripts and played supporting roles as well. Looking at the huge number of independent westerns he directed in the mid-twenties, the casual observer would get the distinct impression that McGowan slept upright with his megaphone in position, shouting directions in his sleep. Unfortunately, many of the pictures he directed lacked the finesse exhibited in those he made with Cody.

After completing the IPC contract in 1925, Bill was signed by Pat Powers's Associated Studio for more westerns, this time to be released by Associated Exhibitors, and although the production quality slipped a bit in these films, *"The Galloping Cowboy"* and *"King of the Saddle"* continued in the rough, tough Bill Cody vein.

Cody stayed that way in nearly every western he made.

Bill's career reached its high point in 1927–28 when he formed Bill Cody Productions, arranging distribution through Pathé. Cody took over the writing and direction of his own pictures, injecting a refreshing note of comedy in films like *Laddie Be Good*, a rather unusual parody of the melodramatic westerns he had been making and one that followed along the lines of the early Doug Fairbanks spoofs. According to his father's will, ranch hand Cody arrived in Chicago to begin the life of a gentleman of inherited wealth. Quickly bored stiff with his new life, Bill looked around for ways to liven it up, and in the process he turned the estate into a full-blown western ranch, dressing his servants in boots, chaps and ten-gallon hats. Of course, his next-door neighbor happened to be an attractive young lady whose scheming father refused to allow Cody to court her; at the same time, he sought to steal Bill's land and our hero found the excitement he wanted—winning the girl's hand and teaching her father not to trifle with a cowhand.

Unfortunately, Pathé was gasping for life in 1928 and dropped all feature releases when its production schedule was adopted for 1928–29. Cody closed his company and rode over to Universal, where he costarred with former Christie comedienne Duane Thompson in a group of westerns and "underworld" pictures in an attempt to survive the onslaught of sound. Bill also made a few oaters for Monogram in the early thirties, but the Hollywood range was flooded

It didn't pay to tangle with Dynamite Bill Cody . . .

If you did, you were asking for trouble from The Arizona Whirlwind.

Sometimes Bill had to force the issue just slightly to get the answers he needed. Our villainous friend will have a sore tummy when **The Arizona Whirlwind** finishes with him.

Margaret Hampton and Bill in The Arizona Whirlwind.

Bill believed in taking every precaution. A small man, he liked to disarm the big rattlers before cutting them down to size.

as never before with western actors and the competition was overwhelming. Taking to the road during the thirties and forties as a member of the Downie Brothers Ranch Wild West Show, he occasionally returned to the screen in the off-season. His final ap-

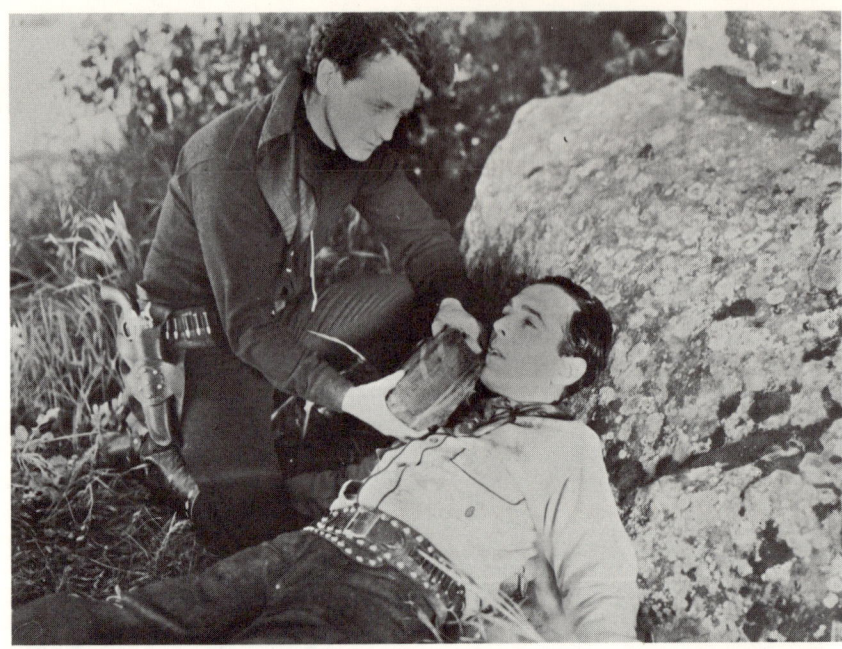

Sometimes Bill had to revive his adversary in order to get the truth. If it isn't forthcoming, pity the poor villain.

Cody liked the largest villains that casting could provide. In this posed still, note how the one on Bill's shoulders is helping to support himself with his feet on the wall of the set.

Bill is having a bit of fun in Laddie Be Good.

Bill Cody and his son in Frontier Days, *1934.*

pearance before the camera came in RKO's *Joan of Arc*, just before he passed away in January 1948.

Although Bill Cody never really made it into the big time as a western star, his pictures were nontheless enjoyable and fast-moving, putting many of his contemporaries to shame with their strong stories and a rigid upholding of the code of honor that most of us who remember tend to associate with the early westerns. His athletic prowess always guaranteed that his fans would receive their money's worth, with none of the romantic hokum of helpless heroines to interfere with the real business at hand—bringing law and order to the Old West.

Lester Cuneo

(THE SMILING DAREDEVIL)

Obscurity came to many of the leading men who starred in the silent westerns, but few were forgotten as quickly as *The Smiling Daredevil*, Lester Cuneo. Although he had only recently completed a group of eight independent westerns for Ward Lascelle Productions, Cuneo was virtually a stranger at the time of his death in November 1925. He was never one of the big western stars, but anyone who saw Lester in action certainly remembers his films, and while today he ranks far below many of his contemporaries of the early twenties, Cuneo had something that attracted. It might have been his distinguished features, the rapid pacing and fast action of his successful films—or perhaps, more likely, it was Lester Cuneo's acting ability that set him apart in the memories of western fans.

While Cuneo's studio biography placed his birth in the Indian Territory in 1888, he was actually the Chicago-born son of immigrant Italian parents. His studio biography also proclaimed him to be a graduate of Northwestern University and its Law School, but in reality Lester spent some eight years in stock and repertoire before entering pictures as an actor-director with the pioneer Selig Polyscope Company in Chicago around 1910. After three years with Selig, Lester disappeared for a few months. He later claimed to have spent the time in Bliss, Oklahoma, as a member of the Miller Brothers 101 Ranch Show. In view of his later affiliation with Joe Miller, this may well be true; but nearly every western actor claimed the 101 Ranch Show as a part of his professional experience, much the same way that every Tom, Dick and Harry who worked for Keystone later proclaimed himself as a member of the original Keystone Cops. But reappearing in Chicago with Essanay in 1914, his work in support of Francis X. Bushman brought Cuneo's name to the attention of reviewers, who began to comment on his excellent portrayals in *Grustark, Under Royal Patronage* and other Bushman-Bayne pictures.

The Smiling Daredevil.

When Bushman left Essanay to join Fred Balshofer's Quality Pictures, Cuneo went with him and was frequently seen in the Quality-Metro productions of 1915–16. Balshofer then formed the

Silver Spurs *with Francelia Billington, his wife.*

Yorke Film Company in 1916 to produce features starring Harold Lockwood and May Allison, a popular romantic team of the period. Lester moved his supporting roles over to Yorke, earning special praise for his portrayal of Donald Smead in *Pidgin Island,* a moving story of the sea and one of Lockwood's big hits of 1917.

Cuneo took time out to star in Uncle Sam's big production in France during 1917-18, rising from the ranks to become a lieutenant before his discharge. He returned to Hollywood, this time as a heavy. By 1920, Lester was well on his way to reestablishing his career, supporting Tom Mix and playing an important role in James Cruze's Realart hit, *Food For Scandal.* To this point, Cuneo had not specialized in any particular type of film, but after marrying Francelia Billington, Lester gravitated toward the western-adventure film, and in 1921 he launched Lester Cuneo Productions, bankrolled by Russell-Grevier-Russell Distributing Company. His five-reel features (*Lone Hand Wilson, The Ranger and the Law, Pat O'The Range*) were distributed on the independent market by the Capital Film Company, which R-G-R now owned. Grace Gordon was his feminine lead in the first few, but was replaced by Miss Billington, a veteran actress from the days of Majestic, American and Thanhouser, and former leading lady for William Russell.

While the Capital series established Lester Cuneo as a hard-

A scene from Lone Hand Tex, *one of Lester's final starring films for Ward Lascelle Productions. The comic element in this series destroyed Lester's image, already weakened by poor scripting and direction.*

fighting rider of the West, his first really successful and most popular series began in late 1921. These eight cyclonic five-reelers were supervised by Charles W. Mack and produced by the Ovid M. Doubleday Production Company, with Henry McCarty and Leo Meehan contributing much of the story material for programmers such as *Blue Blazes, Blazing Arrows, The Devil's Ghost,* and *Silver Spurs.* Filmed in the vicinity of Mt. Baldy, there was little that was original in the plots of these films, but Irving M. Lesser's Western Pictures Exploitation Company made a killing in the independent market with them.

One of the most popular, *Blue Blazes* featured Lester as Jerry Connors, a champion prizefighter who saved the mortgaged ranch of Mary Lee (Miss Billington) and whipped the crooked foreman in a thrilling slug-fest among the flames of an oil fire on the ranch. The "Strongheart" model served Cuneo well in *Blazing Arrows*, a story of racial conflict surrounding a college-educated Indian who tried to help a female classmate in distress. While the denouement detracted from the picture's strength by changing Lester to a white man brought up as an Indian, it was an easy way out for the scripters and provided an opportunity for some splendid villainy by Lew Meehan and James O'Neil. *Silver Spurs* found our hero as

Francelia Billington and Lester in Lone Hand Tex.

a New York-based adventurer who went West in search of romance. California provided the setting—a beautiful Spanish girl who had been defrauded by an unscrupulous half-breed and all the adventure Lester could handle before he regained her property and returned to New York with his new bride.

An immediate hit with western fans in this series, Cuneo's Doubleday features are the ones that come to mind first when Lester's name is recalled today. His striking features, black hair

Gearing himself up for action in Blue Blazes.

and a distinctively noble appearance made him a most acceptable hero and with his large shoulders, a 180-pound frame and a 6' 1" build, Cuneo was more than a match for any screen villain. Yet Lester's career as a leading man stalled and began to slowly wither. He would film *Days of The Buffalo* on the Miller Brothers' 101 Ranch in Oklahoma, a story of a famous Oklahoma massacre which featured Joe Miller (one of the Miller brothers) and Helen Farnum in his support, but it was back to secondary roles in 1922–23. One of Lester's final appearances in a first-run picture was a supporting role in Metro-Goldwyn's *The Eagle's Feather*, starring James Kirkwood, whose obscurity today nearly matches that of Lester.

Cuneo came back to starring roles in a 1923–24 series he never should have filmed. Ward Lascelle, who had been an assistant director at Fox, had entered the independent production field in the early twenties. *Rip Van Winkle*, with the elderly stage actor Thomas Jefferson, and *Mind Over Motor*, with Trixie Friganza and Ralph Graves, had been early Lascelle successes and were followed by Cuneo's final screen series. In spite of a supporting cast which included John "Shorty" Hamilton, Alma Deer and Francelia Billington, these features disappointed exhibitors and fans alike with their woefully weak story lines and inept direction, both by an unknown, W. Adcock. *Western Grit, Lone Hand Tex, Two-Fisted Thompson*—

The Masked Avenger.

The Ranger and the Law.

they failed uniformly and miserably. One dejected exhibitor fairly well summed it up when he commented on *Range Vultures* in the August 29, 1925, issue of *The Moving Picture World*: "Poor old Lester! This is the last of a second series for this star and we can truthfully say that his first series was far superior. Even the strong admirers of Cuneo complained! Cuneo, with a high-class action director, surely could deliver the goods."

At 37, a dejected Lester Cuneo had seen his star rise briefly and fall with shattering rapidity, and on November 2, 1925, he took his own life. To those who remember seeing the Lester Cuneo of the Doubleday series, few doubt that his magnetic screen personality would have carried "The Smiling Daredevil" much closer to the top, had he been featured by one of the larger production firms and backed with adequate writing, direction and career guidance.

Bob Custer

Bob Custer was an unusual western star in every sense of the word; he couldn't act to save his life, his on-screen performances were stiff and awkward, his physical appearance changed markedly during his career, he was not photogenic and his later pictures were as bad as his acting—yet Custer was popular with western fans of the twenties to a degree which is hard to believe today.

Born in October 1900 in either Kentucky or Colorado, depending upon your source (studio biographies cited Colorado first and later referred to Kentucky, crediting him with a degree from the University there), Custer's route to pictures had a familiar ring—work in a variety of stock companies from Colorado to Massachusetts, which led to the Miller Brothers 101 Ranch Show and then to movies. His screen debut came in 1924 with the *Texas Ranger* series produced by Jesse Goldburg's Independent Pictures Corporation and distributed by FBO. Reeves Eason, one of the top action directors of the period, megaphoned Bob's initial starring picture, *Trigger Fingers*, and it was followed in quick succession by *Flashing Spurs, Man Rustlin', The Fighting Boob* and dozens of others.

By 1927, Custer was able to leave Goldburg and formed his own Bob Custer Productions, grinding out *The Fighting Hombre, Galloping Thunder* and *Terror of The Bar X* as part of a series which brought his association with FBO to a close. This year marked the beginning of a slump in the western's popularity and several established western stars would find it rough sledding into the thirties as a result, but not Bob Custer. Signing with Syndicate Pictures in 1928, he continued the assembly line approach with *Arizona Days, The Silent Trail, On the Divide*—and on, and on, and on, with seemingly no end in sight. But sound finally stopped Bob Custer dead in his tracks; an unbelievable career which appeared to have no end suddenly ran into a brick wall and collapsed. He found work only in the cheapest independent westerns of the thirties and soon faded into villainous roles before disappearing from the screen altogether.

Raymond Anthony Glenn, better known as Bob Custer.

How does one explain the phenomena of a man, whose acting was just short of being ridiculous, reaching the status of starring roles in what were often reasonably good pictures otherwise and could have thus profited no end from his absence? To begin with, Goldburg did not expect the Custer series to last. Pleasantly sur-

Bob's later appearance was perfectly suited for the villainous roles he undertook in the mid-thirties.

prised by the public reception of the initial releases, he began to back Bob's films with better production values and supporting casts. Custer came across on the screen as a likeable but slightly confused leading man, but this could be and was overlooked by fans whose demands were simply for hard riding, rough fighting

Bob Custer and Jean Arthur in A Man of Nerve.

Ambush Valley.

Bulldog Pluck.

Steve Clemente, about to stab Bob Custer in Trigger Fingers.

and straight shooting—all elements found in ample quantities in Bob's FBO films.

But as success gilded the lily, Custer began to put on weight. His features fleshed out sufficiently to destroy any notion that he was photogenic and soon his 6-foot frame was distorted enough to destroy even the illusion of height on-camera, an unfortunate circumstance that also overtook Jack Hoxie. Custer's stern, relentless visage never changed its expression; he marched through film after film like a wooden soldier. Leading ladies were present only for motivation—that is, their ranch had been stolen or they were in other danger from the villainy he had sworn to eradicate. Love interest was nothing more than a pretense and I suspect that even his horse chuckled now and then as Bob peered under his huge Stetson at the palpitating heroine with something less than interest. Occasionally, he showed a gleam of his acting range by cracking a half-smile, but woe to the viewer who sat through a Bob Custer western watching for it—one yawn and all of his waiting might well have been wasted.

Very few of the Custer FBO westerns seem to be left today, but his Syndicate Pictures of 1928–29 are abundant in number and although they tend to distort the composite of Bob Custer, screen

The Fighting Boob *was one of Custer's poorest roles for FBO.*

Bob wasn't much of an actor, but even less a fighter.

hero, such films as *Covered Wagon Trails* and *Arizona Days* do give an insight into what kept Custer afloat on the screen for so long. The former was a smuggling story, with Phyllis Bainbridge entangled in illegal activities because of her smart-alec brother. As a deputy, Custer was known to the gang and thus he decided to work through the girl to learn all he could about its activities. Not surprisingly, she resisted every bit of advice this stranger tried to give her until the very end, when Bob finally administered a sound whipping to all concerned. In *Arizona Days,* he again portrayed an undercover agent, this time on the trail of cattle rustlers, courtesy of the Cattleman's Association. Once again, he was unable to make any headway with Peggy Montgomery, who, although basically a nice girl, preferred the outlaw leader (J. P. McGowan) to Mr. Custer.

This problem with his leading ladies was not peculiar to the Syndicate features; it dated back almost to the beginning of his career. In *The Fighting Boob* (1926), one of Bob's war buddies was called West to help his uncle save the family ranch from falling into unscrupulous hands. His friend, a victim of a German gassing in France, was not up to the trip and Custer stepped into his shoes, posing as the nephew. The rather vague plot contained several

Bob Custer presented an awesome appearance with his mono-expression; he ruined that atmosphere when he moved.

On the Divide.

Former serial hero Walter Miller has it in for Bob in Parting of The Trails.

unexpected and unexplained developments including a sudden and unexpected shift in the love interest, and hero Bob lost the girl to the real nephew—before he was even identified. There is a distinct possibility that his script writers simply didn't like Bob Custer.

Now comes the question of why these westerns were not laughed out of the theatres by audiences, which by this time were composed mainly of children. That's part of the reason; the remainder rested in the fact that Bob Custer exemplified the image of the stalwart hero who could not be led astray from his assigned duties—he spanked the leading ladies with regularity and seldom lost a fight with the villain. When he did, it was but a ruse to build the bad man's ego to a point of overconfidence, at which time Bob would step back in and cut him down to size. In short, Custer portrayed a literal interpretation of the good guy, just as fans expected him to.

Like Jack Perrin, Bob Custer was a comfortable hero in that he was completely predictable. There was never any doubt that he would win out in the end and even the seemingly insurmountable odds he usually faced could not shake the audience's confidence—Bob Custer *would win*. His Syndicate pictures came close to the

Hair Trigger Baxter.

end of a career which never should have been and played in a diminishing market of neighborhood houses; Custer had been fortunate in that his popular period at FBO also coincided with the years of the silent western's peak demand. Beyond this, there can be no excuse for Bob Custer's stardom; even his horse was a clinker.

★★★

William Desmond

The silent motion picture was really quite kind to many actors from the legitimate stage. Not that it necessarily made stars of them all, but the pay was often quite a cut above their earnings behind the footlights and staying in one place long enough to make a picture was a welcome, almost idyllic existence for many who had tired of the interminable one-night stands. In the early days of the picture business the legitimate actors had snubbed the screen as being beneath their dignity, but money sometimes talks louder than pride and when the Triangle Film Corporation was formed in 1915, many attitudes changed overnight. Its offer of phenomenal salaries to certain stage stars, and substantial ones to those of lesser stature, brought Broadway to the silver screen.

The western genre, which really didn't require too much in the way of acting talent to allow one the luxury of just getting by, found a place for several stage personalities who were unable to make the transition from footlights to camera with ease, but a few, like William Desmond, hit the jackpot in a big way. Fortunate in that he was something of an accomplished screen actor, the barrel-chested Irishman had carved a niche for himself in society dramas between 1916–21, but it wasn't until he discovered the West that Bill Desmond could truthfully say that his career really began to move. And even then, it wasn't the West alone that made the difference; Bill had completed a few westerns for Jesse D. Hampton and Metro but real stardom was denied him until Universal beckoned.

In the remaining eight years of his silent-film career, Desmond became well known to western fans, primarily as a serial hero. In his mature forties, when serial stardom made him a marquee favorite, Bill's physique was well-suited for chapter play heroism, although the camera made him appear a bit stocky and shorter than he really was, reducing his effectiveness as a romantic lead (something he wisely shied away from). Projecting the older, experienced brother image, tender scenes of Desmond wooing his leading lady

Bill first came to the attention of western fans at Triangle. Starring mostly in society dramas, he occasionally appeared in western roles, as in Bill Hart's 1916 The Dawn Maker, *with Blanche White.*

were kept to a minimum, and even sometimes played for light comedy. He was most effective when cast as a construction engineer or shirt-sleeved newspaperman, for Bill's heavy eyebrows and square face lent to these roles a realism he was never quite able to capture in his earlier society pictures. Here was a man whose every appearance was ideally suited for outdoor action dramas.

Desmond menaces Ed Brady in Deuce Duncan.

Bill points the way in Fightin' Mad, *his own production for Metro release in 1921.*

Coming Attraction slides portrayed Bill in an appropriate western stance.

Working hand-in-glove with stuntmen Jean Perkins, Joe Bonomo, Paul Malvern and George Fiske, he created many awe-inspiring thrills on celluloid and some of the best cliff hangers ever to come from the Universal assembly line, never straying far from the western range in the process. When he first came to the serial, Bill was physically capable of doing his own stunts, but for a poor sense of timing which betrayed him in his very first chapter play epic, *Perils of The Yukon*. The 44-year-old actor spent quite some time recovering from injuries incurred when a 50-foot dive into an icy river failed to work out as planned, and from that time on Universal provided a double for all of the strenuous scenes. As Bill neared 50, he put on quite a bit of weight which the camera accentuated unfavorably, but it didn't seem to matter to his fans. Whether disguised as *The Riddle Rider, The Mystery Rider* or *The Vanishing Rider,* he fooled no one except the villains; but the small fry in the audiences sat on the edge of their seats week after week.

Desmond was also a busy hero. Under contract to Universal for serials and features, he spent his time between Universal assign-

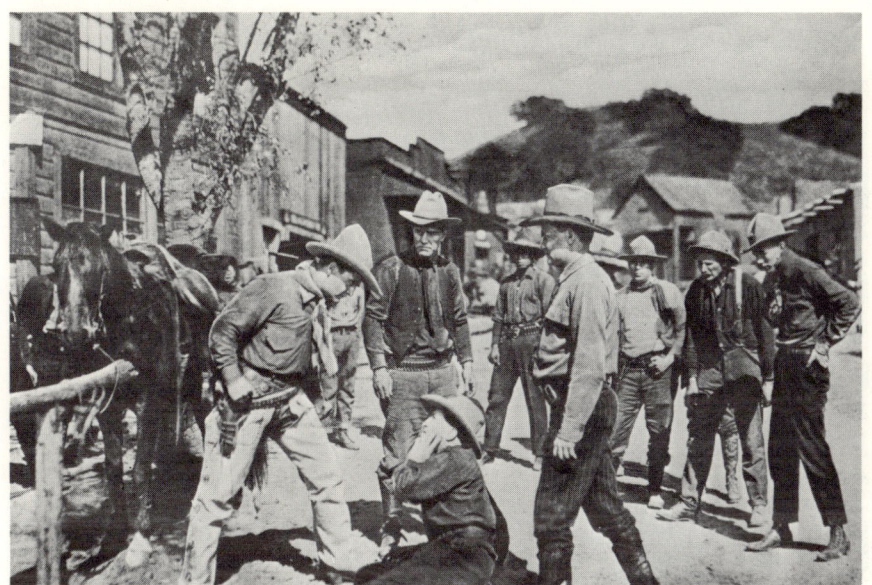

During his early screen career, Bill was as rough and tough as they came . . .

But as the advancing years took their toll, Desmond tended to threaten severely before taking action.

Bill Desmond was always good for a scrap, whether in a bar room (The Winking Idol) . . .

ments co-starring with Helen Holmes in five-reel westerns for Jesse Goldburg's Independent Pictures Corporation and touring vaudeville houses with a western act featuring his second wife, actress Mary MacIvor. His western domain extended from the land of the big timber (*Blood and Steel*) and the oil fields of Oklahoma (*The Riddle Rider*) to the Canadian Northwest (*Perils of The Yukon, Shadows of The North*) and Bill was equally at home regardless of where the script writers chose to hang his hat.

Although strongly melodramatic in nature, his stories seldom showed much originality, but occasionally one came along with an unusual twist. In *McGuire of the Mounted*, Desmond played a NWMP officer framed by a gambler and drugged. Knowing of his love for a poor French-Canadian girl, the gambler then arranged to have Bill married in his drugged state to a dance hall girl—the ultimate shame to the uprighteous Mountie, who was unable to remember just what had happened to him. The villain then tried to have the wanted man framed once again, just for good measure. This time, it was for the murder of another NWMP officer but, treated like a decent woman for the first time, his new wife exposed the plot in an effort to save Bill's life. This act cost the kindly soul her own, but freed Desmond to marry the girl of his choice at the end.

Bill's biggest hit and perhaps the Universal serial most desired today by collectors was *The Riddle Rider*. Directed by William Craft in 15 episodes, this 1924 cliff hanger found a small western community endangered by lawless oil barons and land grabbers. Just when it seemed that all was lost for the decent element, a mysterious rider in black swept out of the night, wreaking havoc among the unscrupulous who sought to rule the town. Not even Eileen Sedgwick, the principal organizer of the "good folks," knew that their benefactor by night was her suitor by day, the local newspaper editor. Why she was unable to see around his moustache disguise is beyond understanding today, but 1924 audiences accepted it as sufficient. To Desmond went the distinction of having created one of the two silent chapter play heroes (excluding Tarzan) whose further adventures were recounted in a sequel (*The Return of the Riddle Rider*). The other was criminologist Angus Blake, whose debut in *Blake of Scotland Yard* (1927) featured Hayden Stevenson in the title role; Crauford Kent portrayed Blake when he returned in "The Ace of Scotland Yard" (1929).

Or a newspaper office (The Riddle Rider) *with Eileen Sedgwick lending moral support.*

Bill's fight for possession of the telegraph poles in Strings of Steel *was short and decisive.*

Fifty-two years old when sound put the silent western into limbo, Bill Desmond went into the thirties playing supporting roles, sometimes as the sheriff, but quite often as a heavy. This change of status was shared by other serial heroes. Walter Miller of the very popular Miller-Ray Pathé cliff hangers found himself in similar circumstances almost overnight. But gradually the roles became smaller and fewer, and on November 3, 1949, "The Riddle Rider" rode into the Valley of Death for the last time.

Desmond defended Eileen Sedgwick against charges that she spied for a rival telegraph company in Strings of Steel.

In the thirties, Bill was seen in supporting roles, usually as the villain or sheriff. This scene is from Superior Talking Pictures' Way of the West, a Rough Rider Western. From left to right, Bobby Nelson, Bill Patton, Desmond, George Kesterson (Art Mix) and Wally Wales.

When Bill was not romancing Ethlyne Clair as The Vanishing Rider . . .

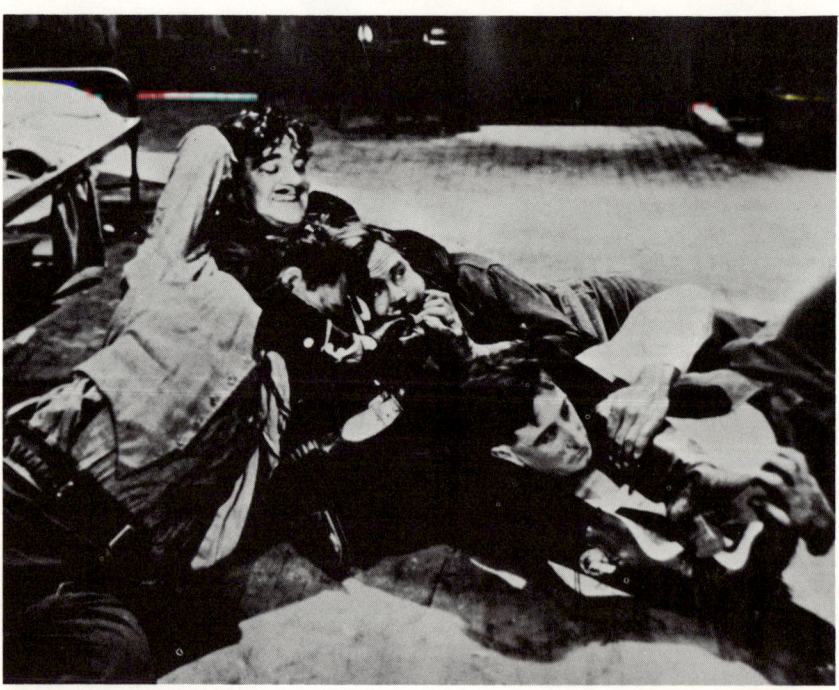

He was busy blocking the Bradley gang in their efforts to steal the gold bullion.

Few of the youngsters who grew up with the Saturday matinees in the thirties were aware that Bill had once shared monthly billing with Hoot Gibson and Jack Hoxie on the Universal range, and so over the years both Desmond and his reputation fell into obscurity. His only pictures available today for screening by the general public are a few of the independent westerns, certainly not a fair reflection of Bill's screen work; but fortunately, some of his better pictures have been preserved by private collectors, and watching these one becomes convinced that William Desmond deserved a better fate.

William Duncan

Few western or serial stars endeared themselves to screen fans more than a 5' 10" pipe-smoking Irishman named William Duncan. His pictures were not extraordinary and although many of his starring roles repeated the same slender story thread time after time, Duncan acquired a following of the faithful which has outlived the object of its admiration. And admire seems to be the key word in Bill's case—of the thousands of letters I've received over the years from serial and western fans around the world, few have failed to mention how much the manly Duncan impressed them as kids at a Saturday matinee with the sense of fair play he exhibited on the screen.

Bill's screen career began with Selig around 1911 and he wrote, directed and starred in hundreds of short comedies, dramas and westerns before finding stardom with Vitagraph in a 1917 serial, *The Fighting Trail*. A highly accomplished athlete (Duncan had once operated a physical culture school), Bill was fond of doing his own stunts, and filming them in such a manner that there could be no dispute over who performed them. Once his serial success was assured, Duncan talked Vitagraph president Albert E. Smith into putting him under contract as director as well, and for the five years that he was a top cliff-hanger favorite, Bill exercised near-total control over the production of his films.

Even Duncan's second marriage to Edith Johnson, the original Kodak girl, failed to shake his grasp on the public (as such had with many other film favorites of the period), although many of his small-fry fans would have preferred to have seen Bill tie the knot with Carol Holloway, the heroine in his first three serials. But at that, Duncan fans accepted Miss Johnson as his leading lady, on and off-screen, and paid homage with a flood of coins that made Albert E. Smith's pinched face break out of its sour mold each time he looked at the books.

Fame is ephemeral, especially motion picture stardom, but in Duncan's case it might never have come had Vitagraph not made an

William Duncan

unusual mistake. Buying a "north woods" story from Jack London in 1916, Smith had assumed that it was free and clear of all encumbrances, not knowing that the famed author had written it under commission by William Randolph Hearst and his Cosmopolitan Studio. Hard-pressed for cash, London had simply decided to peddle whatever he could to any interested party and so Duncan returned from location shooting in Northern California to learn that his seven

William Duncan and Carol Holloway, the stars of 1917's **The Fighting Trail.** *Duncan became Vitagraph's most popular serial hero and his western chapter plays captivated youngster fans from 1917 to 1924.*

episodes of footage were worthless—Vitagraph could not release a serial based on a story they didn't really own and Hearst refused to negotiate the rights. After this incident, Smith took great pains to see that his stories were conceived right on the Vitagraph lot by his own contract writers.

Story wasn't quite the best descriptive term for Duncan's scripts; his serials were little more than a series of stunts hung on a con-

William Duncan and Edith Johnson experience a tense moment from The Silent Avenger.

venient incident and nearly all took place in a western construction or lumber camp setting. In addition to nine serials, Bill made quite a handful of program features in the early twenties, most of which were action-packed melodramas, short on story line but strong on the good vs. evil theme. One of his better films, *The Silent Vow*, had a RCMP background, with Duncan playing a dual role as father and son. The story opened as the young Mountie's wife deserted her family to run away with a notorious renegade and then flashed ahead 20 years. The Mountie is now an Inspector and his son a Corporal. The father is killed arresting his old enemy and the son becomes the instrument of revenge.

In the course of five reels, 12 persons died a violent death; but as most were of the "unruly element," fans agreed that they had received their just reward, so this over-emphasized violence raised not an eyebrow. During the manhunt for his father's slayer, the Corporal was captured, bound hand and foot and left in a cabin under guard. In ordinary circumstances, the hero should have been effectively checkmated, but neither Bill nor his writers felt that logic should ruin a good story. Picking up a hammer with his teeth, Bill hopped over to the table and swung it with enough force to lay his captor out cold. With writers like these on his side, how could Duncan

Like all western stars, physical culturist Bill Duncan was in his element whenever a brawl came his way.

possibly lose? Besides such momentary lapses, the film never really explained why it had taken the old Inspector 20 years to locate his mortal enemy, who had lived all the time in a cabin just a half-day's ride (according to the sub-titles) away from the scene of his perfidy.

Youthful fans of Duncan paid little attention to such fine details and inconsistencies, if indeed they ever took note of them. Bill preached the clean, healthy life and made it seem a most desirable path to follow. Evil was black and good was white—it was that simple. And no matter what the odds, good eventually triumphed, enjoying the reward (usually Miss Johnson) sought by evil. In a less complex world, this message came across loud and clear; today, it would be laughed out of the theatre, but kids in the twenties had not been subjected to the mind-warping indecision and insecurities characteristic of today's generation. They believed that if a better world was possible, Bill Duncan's road would take them there. And for a time, it almost seemed that it could.

But when Vitagraph determined that its survival rested in besting Paramount's feature production, serials were dropped and the Duncans moved over to Universal. The free and easy atmosphere of Bill's Vitagraph unit was quickly replaced by the air of suspicion which pervaded Uncle Carl Laemmle's domain—company auditors constantly prowled about, demanding continual explanation of the unit books and gradually making life miserable for all concerned.

While set in a western locale, Duncan's pictures were not westerns of the stereotyped "shoot-'em-up" variety....

....but adventure stories integrated with basic elements of the silent western, as in "Man of Might".

Duncan and Edith Johnson face Joe Bonomo and company in Wolves of The North.

While Duncan had managed to surround himself with a fairly constant and quietly competent group of technicians and supporting players at Vitagraph, they now began to drift away and the handwriting was there for all to see—the old days were over and so Duncan ended his starring career voluntarily.

Both he and Edith Johnson left the screen in 1925, and toured vaudeville houses before eventually retiring. The Duncans raised their family and led a quiet, happy life together, punctuated only by the few small roles that Bill occasionally undertook in sound films, until death took him in 1961. Bill Duncan's brand of screen fare was professional, entertaining and non-pretentious, a far cry from the "sophistication" Hollywood passes off today as "art." Regrettably, very little of his work has survived over the years, but for those of us who were captivated by his vigorous portrayals, the stalwart Irishman remains vivid in our dimming memories.

William Fairbanks

One of the fascinating aspects of the silent film was the free and easy way in which production firms were created almost overnight on a small capital investment. Most of these shoestring companies folded almost as quickly as they were formed; other were one-film arrangements brought to life for just this reason, a quick profit and bankruptcy. But a surprising number of careers began this way, and while many fell by the wayside over the years, several became powers with which to reckon in the independent production arena.

Westerns or comedies were usually the choice of the Poverty Row producers—they required no expensive sets or studios; some firms even operated on location (which simply meant outdoors), taking advantage of the free sets provided by city streets and local ranches. Whatever interior scenes were required could be ganged together and shot in a day or less using rented facilities. Western Feature Productions was such an operation and its claim to posterity is two-fold.

One was Anthony J. Xydias, whose connection with the motion picture industry dated from 1906. Over the span of 15 years, Xydias had built a small exhibition empire in Texas, Louisiana and Mississippi, and in 1921 he entered the production business as secretary and treasurer of F. M. Sanford's Western Feature Productions. Xydias would soon leave Sanford to set up his own shop, releasing dozens of westerns under the banner of his Sunset Productions throughout the mid-twenties.

The other was Carl Uhlman, star of the Western Feature releases and better known to sagebrush fans of the twenties as William Fairbanks. A wandering stage and stock actor from St. Louis, Uhlman was to begin a screen career which, although prolific for a few years, never carried him very close to real stardom. As William Fairbanks, he had the association by name with Douglas Fairbanks, who was rising rapidly in public favor with his rather extravagant screen spectacles, but nothing else in his favor. As a leading man and hero, Bill left quite a bit to be desired; his rugged but shifty appearance more closely fitted character and heavy roles,

William Fairbanks, alias Carl Uhlman.

The Clean-Up.

Reforming the town single-handed sometimes had its disadvantages. From **The Clean-Up.**

Recovered, a dauntless Bill tries again.

The Sheriff of Sun Dog.

and even granting that the hero did not have to be as handsome as Mix, Jones or Wally Wales, Bill never quite came across convincingly on the screen in heroic proportions.

But his films were sufficiently popular in neighborhood houses to keep Fairbanks busy making series for Arrow, Perfection, Columbia and three of Sam Saxe's companies—Camera Pictures, Gotham and Lumas—before settling into character roles in the M-G-M Tim McCoy westerns of 1927–29. Toward the close of his starring career, Bill turned to baseball, prizefighting and society dramas (*Catch As Catch Can*, *A Fight to the Finish*, *The Winning Wallop*) that emphasized his fine physique and athletic ability over his somewhat lesser talent for acting. While many of his pictures were directed by serial kings Ben Wilson and Charles Hutchison, their work behind the megaphone left as much to be desired as Bill's performance in front of the camera, and for action fans the single redeeming feature of his pictures rested in the fact that the story line usually fell apart by reel three, with hard riding and brawling replacing plot for the majority of the film.

In this aspect, Fairbanks excelled and it was just as well, for the thin plot lines were standard western fare which had been overworked during the years to such a point that their successful

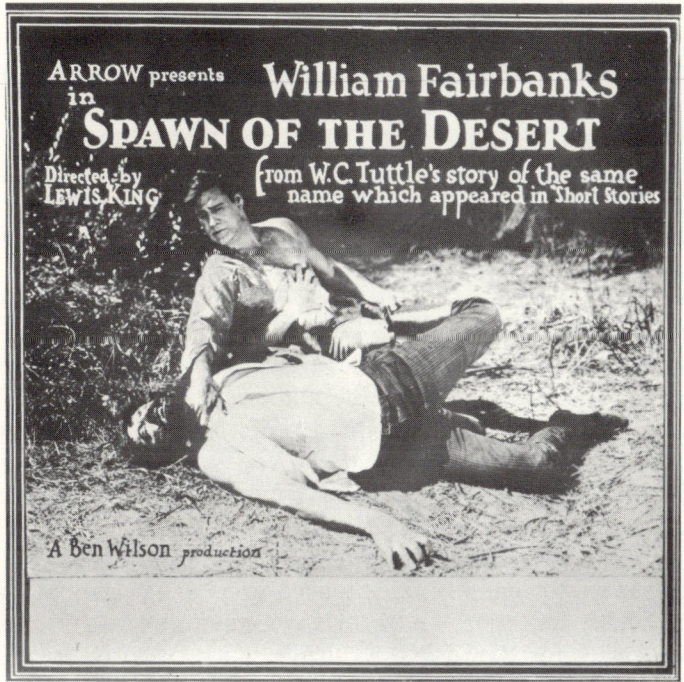
Coming Attraction slides featured Bill in action.

Every Fairbanks western had a "go-for-broke" brawl which pleased his young fans.

use was now dependent upon the leading man's screen personality. Bill had none to speak of, but he certainly could raise a ruckus when it came to a two-fisted, no-holds-barred, knock-down-and-drag-out fight.

In *Montana Bill*, he was a ranch hand framed for cattle rustling and murder by the crooked foreman; *Fighting Bill* found him branded a rustler again, this time shortly after returning home from college. In *Hearts of The West*, Bill changed occupations to become a prospector in love with the wife of a gambler who had double-crossed him and his partner, then tried to steal their claim. These story lines for his Western Features were typical and all resolved with well-placed punches and straight shooting, to the thunderous applause of the small fry in the audience. Fairbanks was sued by Western Features for alleged breach of contract (in the amount of $30,000) when he signed with Ben Wilson. This Arrow series continued in the same vein, but imaginatively titled (*Spawn of the Desert, Sun Dog Trails, The Devil's Door Yard*) and rapidly paced by director Lewis King, they were even more exciting fare for the confirmed western addict; kids tended to be undiscriminating as long as the action was there and Fairbanks gave them a full measure.

His series for Sam Saxe, a former sales executive with Selznick who formed his own production companies, closed out Bill's starring career and coincided with his move into supporting roles. Fairbanks appeared in a large number of films, but was never really well known outside of the theatres which played the cheapest product they could buy. His career was duplicated many times over by dozens of other actors, both western and non-western, who managed to turn a non-acting talent into a profitable living during a time aptly referred to by Professor Edward Wagenknecht as "The Age of Innocence." While communication and transportation were rapidly destroying the agrarian rural society, Saturday's treat for the week in villages and hamlets across the land was William Fairbanks. When you stop to think about it, the realization dawns that even in this supposedly sophisticated age, television hasn't moved the western a great deal farther along the road to art than did the films of Bill Fairbanks and his contemporaries of the silent sagebrush. Can there be a message there?

Franklyn Farnum

(SMILING FRANK)

"Have own horse, western duds and smile—will act." If that advertisement had appeared in movie magazines of the early twenties, every western fan would have immediately recognized it as a reference to one William Smith, better known to patrons of the neighborhood theatres as Frank Farnum. Although often mistakingly assumed by fans and writers to be a brother of the more famous William and Dustin Farnum (a mistake he didn't bother to correct until his later years), Frank had only adopted their last name. Born in Boston around 1883, the gregarious Bill Smith had taken to the boards at an early age, spending a dozen years as a leading man in the productions of Charles Frohman and other stage impresarios before succumbing to the lure of a whirring camera.

While Frank worked for Selig, Universal, Metro, Capellani and many others, his screen career remained mostly undistinguished until 1920, when he signed with Jack Weinberg of the newly formed Canyon Pictures to star with Luella Maxam in a series of 26 short westerns and a serial to be produced by William A. Selig. The serial, *Vanishing Trails*, has not been seen for years, but several of the two-reelers exist. Watching them, the viewer is struck by a dichotomy —in some, Farnum was a complete comic cutup; in others he was the most determined, roughest hombre imaginable and his vigorous portrayals were fashioned in the desolation of a reality in which William S. Hart would have felt perfectly at ease.

Farnum's Canyon westerns (*The Raider*, *The Last Chance*, *Breezy Bob*, *The Uphill Climb*) were melodramatic in nature (when serious at all) but Frank's portrayals were natural, sincere and enthusiastic, and trade reviewers friendly to the independent westerns were fond of comparing him to Bill Hart and Douglas Fairbanks. Frank had his own particular brand of charm to accompany a marked proficiency in riding, fighting and shooting, which were, after all, the essence of the western. Whether romancing

"Smiling Frank" Farnum.

the heroine or trading punches with the bad guys, Farnum carried a mile wide smile that soon earned him the nickname of "Smiling Frank."

Other than the presence of Farnum, the Canyon westerns' greatest interest lies in their early glimpses of one who would become a much greater western star, Charles "Buck" Jones. Whether cast in a straight role or as a ludicrous Indian, Jones provided just the right touch to offset whatever slant Frank chose to embue his characterization with, and if the prints still in existence are typical of the entire Canyon series all 26 must have been enjoyable fare for western fans.

Also something of a jokester off-camera, Farnum's spontaneity on the screen projected well, giving audiences the feeling that he really enjoyed life. His *joie de vivre* took him next to Tulsa, Oklahoma, where the S. M. Smith Merit Studio had just been completed. Hoping to make Tulsa a center of independent western production, Merit had hired Frank, stunt actress Peggy O'Day, Virginia Lee, Al Hart and John "Shorty" Hamilton for a group of westerns. Veteran Francis Ford joined as director and played supporting roles in these humorous westerns (*White Masks, The Angel Citizens, So This is Arizona*). They weren't meant to be especially funny but the script treatments were so poor that Ford and Farnum

Frank strikes a heroic pose, from Wolves of the Border.

Farnum's toothy grin was a familiar sight to patrons of the neighborhood houses.

Humor played a large role in many of Frank's westerns . . .

As did romance . . .

A subtitle from one of his Canyon westerns of 1920.

Frank will soon be sorry he lit that lamp; his back presents a perfect target to the bushwhacker lying in wait outside.

decided to play them for laughs, and at least one, *So This Is Arizona*, turned out to be a rip-roaring comedy. Adapted from an Argosy story, it told the story of an army sergeant who returned from the battlefield without having seen action, only to fall into the middle

But when the going got rough, Farnum was equal to the challenge.

"I'll save the town," says Frank modestly, and he did!

of a range war that was supposed to make the France of 1917 look like a Sunday school picnic, but came off more like a Monday morning ruckus during a kindergarten milk break.

Hart and Hamilton each went on to make their own starring series for Smith, but the Oklahoma climate had its shortcomings and as the resulting films had done little to further his career, Farnum packed his bag at the conclusion of his Merit engagement and returned West to join Phil Goldstone Productions (*Smiling Jim*, *Texas*) and then Jesse Goldburg's Independent Pictures. Frank made a large number of features for IPC (*Caliber .45*, *A Desperate Adventurer*, *The Gambling Fool*) under the direction of J. P. McGowan, but he had passed the high point of his career. Altogether, he starred in over 150 silent westerns but dropped into character and supporting roles in the latter twenties. By the time he retired from the screen in 1956 after an appearance in *Top Secret Affair*, Frank had worked in 1100 films. He then undertook the presidency of the Screen Extras Guild, retiring from that post in 1959, just two years before his death from cancer.

Highly personable and a rather competent actor with a flair for light comedy (although he tended to overplay at times), Farnum's silent westerns were most popular in the small towns during the

Farnum was equally at home playing the gracious host . . .

Or taking orders from the lady boss.

Calibre .45.

period immediately following World War I, when patrons didn't worry too much about a logical story as long as there was sufficient action, comedy and romance to keep them interested. The few Farnum westerns that have survived the years lead one to wonder what he could have done with first-rate stories and direction, for Frank Farnum gave his fans an ample dose of all three, and that was as much as any cash customer could ask for—his money's worth.

Hoot Gibson

(THE SMILING WHIRLWIND)

The last of the silent screen's great western heroes, Ed ("Hoot") Gibson passed away in 1962, and with his death the curtain closed on an era long gone. Hoot, who had picked up his nickname hunting owls in his native Nebraska, was one of that not-so-unusual breed who roamed the silent sagebrush—a genuine cowboy *and* an actor. The thirties would find a different breed sharing the screen with authentic stars like Hoot, Jack Hoxie and Colonel Tim McCoy—sometime actors who wore the garb of a westerner and tried very hard to emulate those whom they sought to replace.

But Hoot Gibson was the real McCoy, as one glance at any of his innumerable films would tell, and he had served a long apprenticeship. Coming to the screen from the rodeo circuits in 1912 after winning the title of All-Around Champion Cowboy at the Pendleton (Oregon) Roundup and a vaudeville tour, Gibson found work as a wrangler and stunt double. The pay was not high but work was steady and not at all dangerous when compared to bulldogging a fast-running 1200-pound steer (Gibson weighed in at 150). Hoot tried hard to make the leap from extra to leading roles, but Hollywood always seemed to be looking the other way and his first wife, Helen (Wenger) Gibson,[1] was much more successful, replacing Helen Holmes in Kalem's long-running series, *The Hazards of Helen*, in 1915.

Hoot continued to double for Harry Carey, taking whatever extra and supporting roles the star could find for him. He once proudly explained that to be an extra was probably the most difficult job in the world; a man had to know how to be shot from a horse and die convincingly. Indians riding bareback took a spill for $2.50 in those days but a cavalryman earned $5.00—it was easier to slide

---

[1] They were married while in Oregon at the Roundup and for an interesting and altogether practical reason—lodging was difficult to come by and preference was given married couples—voila!

Hoot Gibson, as he appeared in 1920.

from the bareback horse than to be "shot" from a horse with a saddle. Universal had just begun to notice the personable young man who was willing and able to do anything to get in front of the camera when World War I broke out and Hoot took a two-year vacation from the screen to serve in the Army's tank corps.

When he returned from the Army in 1919, Universal's expanding schedule of western short subjects finally found a place for him and Hoot was given the lead in his own series in 1919–21. These two-reelers (*Roaring Dan, The Lone Hand, West is Best*) proved so popular that "The Smiling Whirlwind," as he was billed, moved

Hoot at the close of the silent period.

over to features on a trial basis in 1921, teaming with veteran actors J. Farrell MacDonald and Francis Ford, and a fast-rising director named John Ford, to star in *Action*. Hoot never made another short subject. Riding hard and shooting straight, Gibson became a fixture on the Universal range throughout the twenties, bringing a novel touch to the formula western in a lengthy series of well-produced features. Hoot incorporated a dash of humor in his films, but unlike the other sagebrush heroes of the twenties, who relied upon a comic

Gibson came to the top in John Ford's 1921 feature, Action. *Veteran Francis Ford stands at the right.*

sidekick for comedy relief, Gibson handled the humor himself in such a light-hearted way that $14,500 came his way each and every week.

The Gibson touch was most evident in films like *Chip of the Flying U, The Silent Rider* and *The Ridin' Kid From Powder River*; but it wasn't unusual for him to step out of western character in pictures like *Hit and Run, The Sawdust Trail* and *The Thrill Chaser*. *Hit and Run* was typical of these films; Hoot played a baseball-crazy ranch hand named "Swat" Anderson, who hit home runs all over the West, but couldn't field a tumbleweed. Discovered by the major leagues, he became a star player, leading his team to the Series only to be kidnapped by gamblers the night before the big game. Freeing himself, he used a buckboard and a speeding roadster to get back to the ball park just in time to win the game. In *The Sawdust Trail*, Hoot played a collegiate boob wearing horn-rimmed glasses and freshman beanie. These films' one link to the West—

Trimmed.

The Galloping Kid.

Charles Whittaker, Wade Botelar, Steve Reeves, Hoot and Edna Murphy in Ridin' Wild.

and a tenuous one at that—came in their opening scenes; but fans didn't seem to mind. They loved the tow-headed actor whose easygoing manner and boyish charm was accentuated by the camera.

Hoot was fortunate in working for Universal; his pictures were made with a degree of professionalism which many of the other westerns of the period lacked. He was assigned good directors (usually Lynn Reynolds or Ed Sedgwick), above-average stories and his films were carefully edited to maintain a steadily rising pace of action, which held the audience's attention. Universal thought so highly of its top western star that his films were released first as Special Attractions, then Universal Jewels and finally it established the Hoot Gibson Company to make "Gibson Westerns." Over the years, Hoot Gibson became a polished performer and his toothy grin graced the screen in a new release almost monthly. Avoiding gunplay and fancy clothes in his pictures, Hoot also steered clear of saloons; the rugged but clean-cut image which he projected was virtue's own reward.

Toward the close of the silent period, he introduced race cars and airplanes in his pictures, in place of the old reliable horse . . .

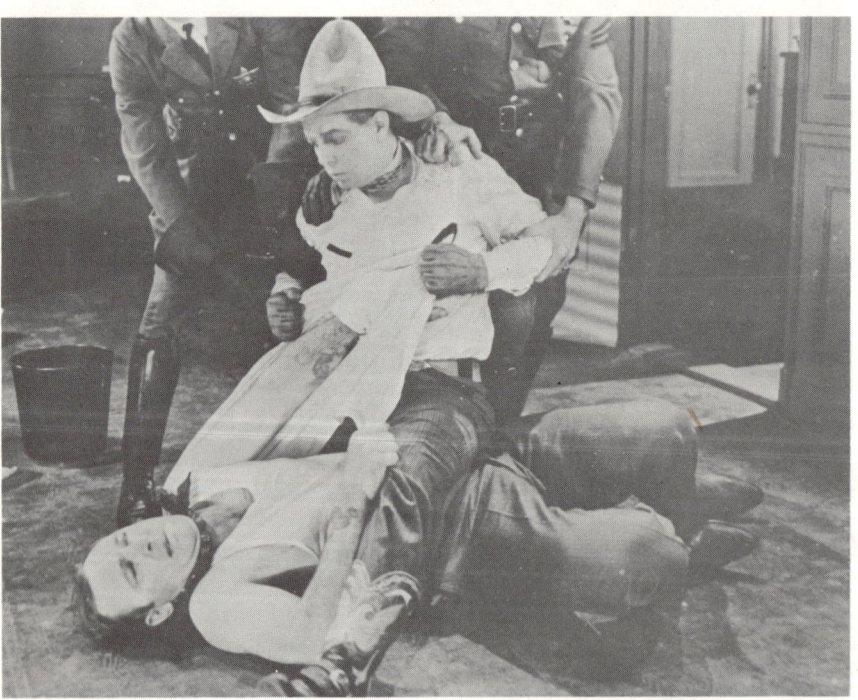

But fans did not seem to mind, as long as he continued to make pictures like King of The Rodeo.

Many of Hoot's features had only a slight connection with the West.

More typical of the films that gave Hoot his reputation as one of the all-time greats, *The Flaming Frontier* was one of his best silent westerns and received critical acclaim as well as earning bushels of money for Universal. Written and directed on a grand scale by Ed Sedgwick, this fictional account of Custer's defeat at the Little Big Horn generally followed the known historical sequence and was well staged. Its lavish battle scenes utilized hundreds of extras and Hoot's portrayal of Bob Langdon, Pony Express Rider,

The Buckaroo Kid.

was a strong one incorporating many fancy stunts and snappy trick riding, and withstood the challenge posed by Dustin Farnum's handling of Custer. *The Flaming Frontier* followed closely after Hoot's comic western, *Chip of The Flying U*, and demonstrated Gibson's ability to follow a humorous role with one of strong dramatic intensity.

Hoot's career weathered the transition from silent to sound films and he continued to ride the range for another 15 years before hanging his spurs up for the final time in 1944. He made scores of talkies in that time, mainly for independent producers, and although his popularity dimmed somewhat toward the end, he had given the singing cowboys a run for their money, and the outcome, while never really in doubt, marked the close of an era. Hoot Gibson was a true gentleman of the West and had created his own very special kind of immortality in the hearts of millions of admirers. How many singing cowboys could claim that?

Texas Guinan

(THE FEMALE BILL HART)

Conquered and settled by daring men and women, the American West gave equal status to the female; not so the cinematic version. Only a handful of women sought stardom in the man's world of Western screen. Somehow, fans didn't identify very well with the female who could settle range wars, clean out the undesirable characters in the town saloon and lock up the vicious desperados who had robbed the local bank, all without help from the stronger sex. Of those who rose to a position beyond providing support to the handsome male hero (or his horse), perhaps the best-remembered was a hefty ex-bronc rider and sometime vaudeville actress, Mary Louise Guinan, better known to posterity and her fans as "Texas."

Coming to the screen in 1917 with the near-defunct Triangle Film Corporation, Texas Guinan's rise to real fame began in 1918 when she signed to make 26 short westerns for the Frohman Amusement Corporation, another independent whose extended existence (for an independent) was coming rapidly to a close. Cliff Smith directed the series and *The Girl of Hell's Agony* and *The She Wolf*, her first two films (with Jack Richardson and George Chesebro in supporting roles) turned out to be five-reel features instead of short subjects. Frohman proved to be an experience hardly satisfying to the would-be actress, and the next year Texas moved to Bulls Eye, turning out another 26 two-reelers—a series that brought her the attention she desired.

Imaginatively titled (*The Night Raider, My Lady Robin Hood, The Desert Vulture*), Texas's films were invariably simple plots which moved quickly, violently and in a straight line from start to finish, equating good and evil as diametrically opposite, with no in-between shades of gray. *Letters of Fire* told the story of the sheriff (Texas), framed by El Tigre to cover up his rustling activities. Accused by her one-staunch supporters, Texas escaped and tracked

Mary Louise Guinan, years before her picture career.

Texas in She Wolf, *one of her Frohman pictures.*

Threatened by Mexican villains in Girl of the Rancho . . .

down the vicious bandit's henchmen, catching them in the act of changing cattle brands. Surprised from behind, our heroine was punished for her audacity by El Tigre, who branded his initials on her bosom before turning the law woman loose. Making her way to the home of a Mexican woman whom she had once befriended, Texas recuperated from the humiliating and painful experience in a few weeks and then set out once more to locate El Tigre and settle the score. This she did in a slam-bang finish which saw her repay the bandit in kind, branding his chest with her initials before being pulled off by the posse, which had fortunately arrived on the scene just in time to round up the rustlers.

Quite short and stocky, almost 30 and far from being an attractive woman, Miss Guinan appeared rather tough and hard-bitten on-screen and her many closeups were painfully revealing, both of this impression and of a gross lack of acting talent. Her overexaggerated gesticulations and grimaces were reminiscent of a technique of screen acting that had died out by 1912; when Texas put on her hat, she put it on with such vigor that fans were certain it wouldn't stop until it reached her knees, but she could ride a horse with the best and tried very hard to live up to her billing as *The Female Bill Hart*. With her pictures playing the cheaper houses around the country, Texas enjoyed a more than modest success during this time, and when her Bulls Eye contract was completed she moved to the Capital Film Company where she set to work on another series of 26 short westerns.

By the time her Capital contract was completed, she was quite well known in the independent field and signed with Victor Kremer for a group of 8 five-reel features directed by Francis Ford. These were finally finished in July of 1921, and the following month Texas organized her own company with the first release scheduled to appear on the state-right market September 15. Mildred Sledge was hired to script the stories and Texas set to work, taking time out only to institute a suit against the Reelcraft Pictures Corporation (distributor of her Bulls Eye series) for the $200,000 that she claimed

Texas takes it philosophically.

As the battle rages below her, Texas registers fear for the safety of a child, hanging by a slender rope out of camera range.

was still owed her from the Bulls Eye contract. Cynics whispered that it was her one recourse to raise sufficient production capital; suffice it to say that only a few of her projected films were actually made. The most interesting thing to come out of this group were the gummed and perforated stamps featuring a variety of photo reductions of Texas and distributed to exchanges and exhibitors for publicity use through the U.S. mail much as we use Easter seals today. And at that, she fudged and used photos taken several years before.

Closing her company, Texas left Hollywood in 1922 to appear in a musical at New York's Winter Garden theater, where a chance meeting with one Larry Fay proved to be the turning point in a career that was moving too slowly to suit the irrepressible Miss Guinan. With Fay as her partner, Texas opened a number of night clubs, which proved to be immensely popular with the habitues of New York night life. In less than a year, her famous greeting ("Hello, Suckers") had earned the ex-movie star a reputed $1 million and she was credited by no less an authority than the *New York*

Everything turned out fine for the smiling Miss Guinan.

While her friends assure her that the rustling charges are false, Texas knows she must prove herself or lose her badge in Letters of Fire.

Captured by El Tigre's henchmen in Letters of Fire, *Texas is branded . . .*

But the villain pays in the end, as Texas returns the favor. Her films were very dramatic and forthright in their battle between good and evil.

Broadway night life was kinder to Texas than her Hollywood makeup man had even been. William Davidson could only admire the new "Queen of the Nightclubs."

Times with creating an entirely new social set—cafe society. As the undisputed "Queen of The Night Clubs," Texas Guinan became symbolic both of The Roaring Twenties and Prohibition—a legend in her own time.

As a result of this greatly enhanced reputation, Texas rode the plains once more in the late twenties, not in new westerns but in the Hollywood version of today's Late, Late television show. Her two-reel westerns (which had never been copyrighted) were recut into single reels, scored with sound effects and dialogue on discs and reissued to the independent market by Melody Productions.

But Texas did make one last film. Late in 1928, Warner Brothers signed her to star in a thinly veiled but partly fictitious feature depicting her career. The Jazz Age was nearly over when Bryan Foy's *Queen of The Night Clubs* was released in early 1929 and while it enjoyed a modest success in the silent houses, the talkie version simply proved that Texas was no more of an actress than she had been earlier in the decade. Existing stills from the film show a new and svelte Miss Guinan, considerably thinner and more attractive than when she rode the cinema range—a tribute both to Texas and Warners' makeup man—but with this picture, the silent film career of Mary Louise Guinan drew to a close.

★★★

Neal Hart

(AMERICA'S PAL)

The lure of the motion picture knew no boundaries; movies drew a highly diverse collection of personalities, and while the room at the top was limited there were many lesser degrees of stardom to be enjoyed; and below that existed the domain of the supporting actor. Although character actors found their staying power to be considerably greater than that of the stars, it was natural that, given the opportunity, they preferred to become leading men. One from the ranks who made the transition when touched by the magic wand became "America's Pal" for almost a decade before tumbling back in Cinderella-fashion to supporting roles and bit parts.

A native of Richmond, New York, Cornelius A. Hart Jr. claimed to have a degree in civil engineering from Pennsylvania's Bucknell University but must have turned his back on the field, for he appeared in Wyoming as a ranch hand around the turn of the century. Supposedly a deputy sheriff in Manville, a brand inspector for Converse County and a U.S. Marshal in the several years he spent in Wyoming, Neal joined the Miller Brothers 101 Ranch Show, touring the country as a roper and bulldogger. The trail's end was Los Angeles, where Hart, Joe Rickson and several others quit the show for the easy money paid by the movie producers. Fascinated by the possibilities of movie-making, Neal decided to stay with it and spent the next 3 years in the relative obscurity of supporting roles (*Liberty, A Daughter of the USA, The Lion's Claws*).

Needing someone in late 1916 to star in a short western he was to direct, George Marshall looked over the available faces on the Universal lot and picked the balding Neal Hart, then in his late thirties. As soon as it became clear that he had a firm grasp on the ladder of stardom, Neal soon affected all the airs of a real

character. The balding scalp suddenly sprouted a luxurious growth of store-bought hair, and as he moved into feature-length productions under his mentor's tutelage Hart saw his salary climb from $5.00 a day to $500 a week. Watching George Marshall closely, Neal learned the fundamentals of writing, directing and acting, and by 1919 was ready to undertake his own company. Setting up shop

Neal in 1917, after George Marshall brought him from an unknown to leading roles in Universal westerns.

in Wyoming, Neal produced *When the Desert Smiled* and sold it for Arrow release.

L. S. Barnhard's Chicago-based Capital Film Company then contracted to release the output of the companies formed by Al Jennings, Texas Guinan, Helen Gibson and Neal Hart on the independent market and acquired the services of Lester Cuneo in 1920. With these five names, Capital had one of the largest aggregations of two-reel westerns and features available to the state-right buyer and proceeded to make the most of its product by advertising exten-

Universal's Naked Fists, *1918.*

sively. Because of this, Neal Hart's name soon became well-known to young movie-goers, and "America's Pal" was on his way. Crammed with action and adventure, his western shorts (*Out of The West, The Square Shooter, Bare Knuckle Gailagher*) played the neighborhood houses, winning him a matinee audience whose loyalty would remain for over a decade.

When the Capital series was completed in 1920, Hugh Woody of Pinnacle Productions in Glendale signed Neal to do a half-dozen five-reel features with Janis June, to be released through Eddy Eckels's Independent Film Association. Another, and more intensive, advertising campaign was begun, culminating with the appearance of a full-page advertisement of Neal Hart and his Pinnacle films in the 1921 telephone directories of every major city in the country. Neal's first film, *Hell's Oasis*, was released October 20, 1920, and was followed by a new feature every six weeks. The Pinnacle Productions were interesting examples of the typical independent

Northwest Mounted Police roles were Neal's favorite. **Tangled Trails** *was his first feature for Steiner in 1921.*

A frame enlargement from **The Fighting Strain,** *with Neal as the Mountie.*

The Lure of Gold.

westerns of the early twenties; story and continuity definitely took second place to the dramatic action and thrill sequences, which were guaranteed to keep the kids' eyes glued to the screen. Not by any wild stretch of the imagination could Neal be considered an actor, but this was hardly a requirement in his type of western. Suffice it to say that he rode tall in the saddle.

Skyfire, his second release, was a Northwest Mounted Police picture, with Neal as a heroic and seemingly invincible Mountie, a role he particularly liked to enact. Pursued by the villains in one sequence, he rounded the bend and leaped from his mount's back, sailing over the cliff and down into the boughs of a tree, which served to break his fall and allowed our hero to scramble down the tree to safety. Recovering from their momentary surprise, the villains regrouped, thinking Neal to certainly be unconscious, if even alive, after such a fall. After attaching a rope to a saddle, they started the perilous journey down the cliff to finish him off, but as fate (and a willing script writer) would have it, the rope broke and they fell right into Hart's hands. But then, everyone knew that the NWMP always got its man. Filled with action of this nature, Neal's Pinnacle films were miniature serials and his devoted followers became devout.

Rangeland.

Following his Pinnacle series, Neal formed the Neal Hart Production Company, and enlisting the temporary assistance of actor-director Paul C. Hurst, he began a lengthy association with William Steiner, who marketed several good series of independent feature westerns in the mid-twenties. At this point in his career, Hart was approached to return on a contract basis to Universal and major release of his films, but the increased salary and regimentation required by such a move would not have offset the sacrifice of his freedom to do as he pleased. Neal was top hand where he was, making a very nice living while writing, directing and starring in his own films, made on location in Texas or wherever else his fancy took him. He did, however, star in a few of the Universal western short subjects of 1923–24.

Neal's relationship with Steiner produced a rather long series of uneven but interesting westerns (*The Devil's Bowl, South of the Northern Lights, The Fighting Strain*) and, although the names changed (Ambassador Pictures, New-Cal Film Corporation), served to occupy his time during the remainder of the silent period. Hart had several definite advantages over his competition in state-right westerns; he was a handsome devil and cut a dashing figure on-screen, even at his age. Realizing his own limitations as an actor, Neal refused to let his screen characterizations become clouded in maudlin love scenes, preferring to pay strict attention to the business at hand—riding, fighting, shooting and helping the law keep order on the celluloid range. He left the acting to a reasonably competent stock company of supporting players. His stories were often routine, but occasionally one came along with a touch of the unusual, like his 1923 *The Secret of The Pueblo*.

This was the story of a large ranch, potentially very valuable but presently worthless because of a lack of water. The various attempts by unscrupulous elements to acquire the land by any means and the presence of a band of mysterious Indians, who possessed the knowledge of where and how a vast supply of water could be found, furnished the basis for the action. An atmosphere of suspense surrounded the Indians and the result was in keeping with Neal's fast-paced adventures. Seen today, *The Secret of The Pueblo* is strongly impressive for an independent western, both in treatment

Rangeland.

Neal and Gladys Hampton in Tangled Trails.

of what could easily have become a trite plot and in the photographic effects of which Neal was fond. While the scenery was not on the scale of a Tom Mix or Jack Hoxie feature, its photographic rendering by Jacob Badarraco was well above that of the competition.

Neal ventured into the serial realm in 1926 with *The Scarlet Brand*. Little is known about this New-Cal release; chapter synopses were not reviewed in the trade papers and no prints are known to have survived, but judging from the serial-like construction of many of Hart's features, it should have been one of the more exciting chapter plays of the year. When queried about *The Scarlet Brand* recently, its author, Arthur Henry Gooden, replied rather lamely, "My Lord, it's been over 40 years now and I'm afraid I can't help you. I wrote so many for Neal and also for the boys at Universal that they're all a blur now, but I can tell you this—none were outstanding or I would have remembered them."

The declining independent market, his advancing age and an uncertainty about the advent of sound brought an end to Neal's starring career; the clock had struck midnight and the Cinderella hero, created by George Marshall, returned to supporting roles, like so many other silent sagebrush heroes. It was ironic that after so many years of independence, Hart finally found it necessary to surrender his creative control in order to work, but appropriate that "America's Pal" made his final screen appearance in Warner Brothers 1949 oater, *The Younger Brothers*; he died at the age of 70 on April 2, 1949.

William S. Hart

Ironically, the man considered to be the foremost exponent of the western film down through the years was not a native westerner, but a Shakespearian actor from Newburgh, New York, whose early life and later travels through the West had given him definite ideas concerning its historical reality. Highly critical of the way in which movie producers were depicting the West and its heritage in their pictures, a determined William S. Hart took up the cudgel in 1914, putting his conception of what the West should be on film for Thomas H. Ince.

Meeting with a success far beyond that which Bill Hart felt he had any good reason to expect, his quick acceptance by the public soon placed him in the role of expert, who preached of a hot, grimy and desolate countryside, peopled by sober humans very similar in emotion and nature to their urban counterparts of the 19th century. The romanticism common to other westerns of the period was an element alien to Hart's interpretation, yet in itself the drab and stark existence he brought forth in his pictures soon became a negative image of the very stereotype Bill had sought to destroy. Carried to its logical conclusion in his later features, its validity was as questionable as that which it replaced.

And yet, there was a truth in his approach—it was the West as Hart remembered it, with all of the disagreeable aspects of life common to any pioneering venture. The western format, which had become stylistically settled and accepted by 1914 through default, was the conglomerate work of many men whose knowledge of western life was as unrealistic as Hart's was individual. Bill Hart at least had the advantage of closer acquaintance with his topic than those producers who had risen from the imigrant ghettos to direct the destiny of the world's largest and most influential entertainment medium. Above all else, he possessed a deep and abiding love for western lore and life as he knew and remembered it. The Eastern producers who only a few years before had been

William S. Hart (l) as he appeared in the stage play of Ben Hur *before coming to the screen in 1914.*

Bill Hart, at the close of his career. A scene from **Tumbleweeds**.

store clerks, gamblers, salesmen and furriers could not be expected to have the same approach—they could not have cared less about reality as long as their investment paid off. Hart was interested less in the money than in seeing justice done to a land and era he loved.

I do not mean to imply that William S. Hart does not deserve the recognition which has been heaped upon him during the past 50 years; it is his due if for no other reason than his popularity, which injected a fresh breath into a simple formula on the verge of stagnation. Technically, Hart's pictures can be dissected and shown to be highly effective applications of cinematic story telling in theory, but the more that one watches his films for entertainment, the more depressing the picture this anti-hero painted becomes.

Hart had two distressing qualities about his work which became more pronounced as his career progressed—repetition and sentimentality. Yet he was enormously popular with audiences for nearly a decade, and in that time he created a legend which is as strong today as it was a half-century ago. While kids no longer aspire to be "as quick on the draw as William S. Hart," mere mention of the silent western automatically brings forth Hart's name, just as Pearl White is *the* silent serial queen.

The Return of Draw Egan

Taking the "good-badman" theme often used by Broncho Billy Anderson before him, Hart developed its portrayal into a finely tuned formula, but whenever he broke away from this mold, as in *The Ruse*, *Shark Monroe* and *The Dawn Maker*, the public failed to respond with the same degree of enthusiasm they reserved for *The Return of Draw Egan*, *Hell's Hinges* and *The Toll Gate*. Directing his own pictures, Bill manipulated the supporting roles

Margery Wilson, William S. Hart in The Return of Draw Egan.

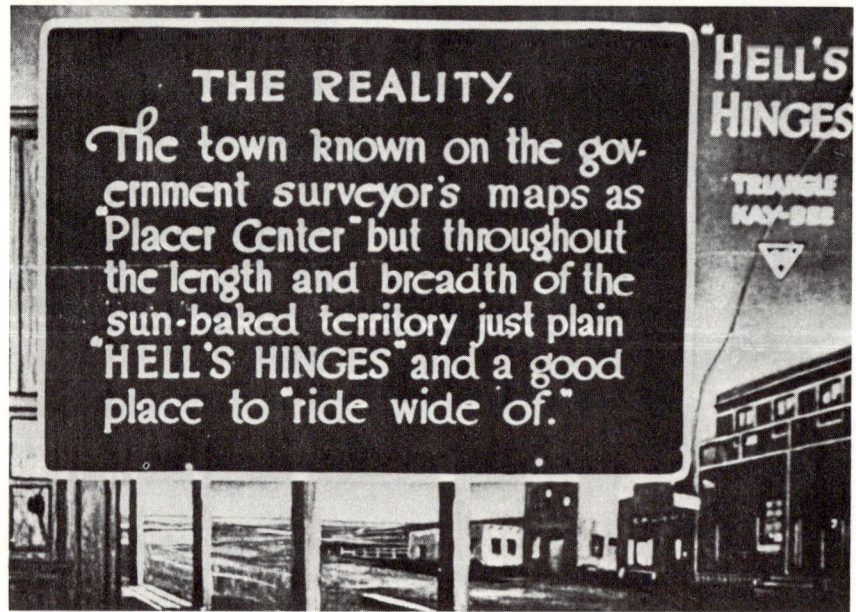
One of the opening titles from Hart's 1916 classic, Hell's Hinges.

A frame enlargement of Hart from Hell's Hinges. *The scene was tinted red for emphasis.*

Border Wireless

around his own, keeping himself the central figure in the story as much as possible and bringing the camera in for many close-ups. It was this technique which broke away from the traditional western and created the intense figure of Hart so well remembered by all who ever saw him on the screen. When Bill was challenged in some way, the camera moved in for a close-up, and suddenly Hart appeared on the screen many times larger than life—hat brim pulled down over his slowly narrowing eyes, nostrils flaring slightly with a deep rhythmic breathing—while Bill considered his opponent. Kids shook in their seats as the stern visage of Bill Hart glared down upon them.

While Broncho Billy had popularized the western, and J. Warren Kerrigan's portrayals gave it new directions, there can be no denying that Bill Hart touched the public's nerve in such a way that the western became both a respectable and profitable genre.

Blanche White, William S. Hart, J. Frank Burke in The Dawn Maker, *1916. Hart played Joe Elk, a half-breed Indian who became chief of his tribe and brought Bruce Smithson (William Desmond) from Montreal to build schools, incurring the wrath of his tribe.*

Hart's imposing appearance was heightened by the use of close-ups at a time when other westerns relied mainly on medium shots to carry the action.

The Primal Lure

Hart's respect for womanhood and his leading lady was a part of his screen character, but he also had a tendency to fall in love with her off the screen. Shown here with former Mack Sennett comedienne Mary Thurman, Bill eventually married Winifred Westover.

At least twice before he came to its rescue, the western film had suffered a sharp public reaction at the box-office. Only Tom Ince had been producing above-average frontier stories in 1912–14, but he had no outstanding personality on his player roster at the time. The effect of Hart's arrival on the screen can be compared to the advent of Keystone on the world of screen comedy in 1912–13.

But under the challenge posed by Tom Mix, and to a lesser extent Buck Jones, Hart's popularity began to erode in the early twenties. While it was obvious that the public was ready to abandon his West for the lighter and less realistic interpretation at which Mix had become expert, Bill would not budge. Evolution in public taste had created his opportunity in 1914, but Hart would not willingly acknowledge that a change on his part was necessary to keep the box-office cash register ringing. He chose to attribute the declining receipts of his films to poor exploitation by Paramount, feeling this was Zukor's way of coercing him into changing his

Retiring from the screen after Tumbleweeds, *Bill stayed on the fringe of the industry and served as technical advisor for King Vidor's* Billy the Kid *in 1930. Here he donates one of the original guns used by William Bonney to a youthful Johnny Mack Brown, who would go on to become one of the program western's top stars.*

style. His stubborn refusal cost him first his independence and then his career, as Bill's next film, *Singer Jim McKee,* was the poorest of the Hart westerns and resulted in Paramount laying down the law—from now on the studio would pick the stories and directors for Bill. Feeling that his integrity had been challenged, Bill Hart saddled up and rode out of the Paramount lot for the final time.

Bill made one last picture which United Artists released, *Tumbleweeds*. Unfortunately, it was Hart's reply to Zukor and while the New York reviews and box-office were good, United Artists executives were not impressed. Their attempt to recut it to suit themselves was prevented by Hart but United Artists countered by deliberately sacrificing the film, booking it into small theatres with little profit potential. Hart took the case to court but even though he won the resulting litigation, he lost in the end—the damage had already been done. He estimated a loss of $500,000 in potential profit not earned and retired from the screen. But the legend was firmly established and as the sands of time closed around the silent screen, Hart was one of the few interpreters of the West who survived the obscurity which sound brought to nearly three decades of the western's development.

Helen Holmes

While most of the western stars were properly associated with their horses, Helen Holmes rode a railroad locomotive to fame and fortune at a time when less daring lassies were idolized by an adoring public for their "heroic" exploits. Railroads and the West were closely linked together in the silents and while Miss Holmes spent about as much time on a horse as she did racing about the tops of boxcars, it was the iron horse that would make her name instantly recognizable to fans around the world.[1]

Born to an impoverished family in Chicago, Helen went to work at an early age as a photographer's model, but shortly after she contracted tuberculosis, attributed to many long hours of posing in water-dampened clothes (to hold their shape) in cold studios. About this time, her family bought a home in Death Valley and moved West, only to discover that they had been swindled. Rescued from her plight by Mabel Normand, a friend from her modeling days, Helen was placed on Mack Sennett's payroll and appeared in a number of bit roles at Keystone. But not until she joined Kalem and wed J. P. McGowan, who would become one of the most proficient action directors in the business, did Helen hit her stride.

Her early films for Kalem had centered around the character of a girl telegrapher and proved so popular with fans that Kalem eventually instituted *The Hazards of Helen* series to compete with the great number of serials being produced in the wake of Pearl White's fantastic success with *The Perils of Pauline* in 1914. Forty-eight of the single-reel films had been made when Helen and her husband were lured to Universal in 1915, leaving Kalem with a highly profitable concept and no star. Helen Gibson replaced Miss Holmes and went on to extend *The Hazards'* run to 119 chapters, but that's another story.

---

[1] Readers today may have difficulty understanding it, but American films dealing with railroads and westerns were even more popular in such unlikely places as Japan, if that can be imagined.

Specializing in western and railroad adventures, Helen Holmes became one of the earliest and most popular of the serial queens. This picture was made at the Signal Studio in 1917.

Helen and McGowan had spent only a few weeks at Universal when Samuel S. Hutchison approached the two with an offer to form the Signal Film Corporation and feature Miss Holmes in genuine serials for release by Mutual. Hutchison offered them a

Helen Holmes, in a frame enlargement from an early chapter of The Hazards of Helen.

share of the company in addition to a salary and Helen began the first in a cycle of four western railroad chapter plays which carried her to the top (*The Girl and the Game, Lass of the Lumberlands, The Railroad Raiders* and *The Lost Express*) as a western action heroine in less than two years, with each serial grossing more than the previous one. By 1917, the attractive daredevil's fans were countless and she was the leading rival to Pathé's serial queen, Pearl White. But Mutual collapsed and with it went the Signal Film Corporation.

Helen then went into independent production in 1919 for S. L. Krelberg to produce a chapter play which deviated from the western-locomotive-horse formula, *The Fatal Fortune,* and in one of those difficult-to-understand reversals of public favor, the audiences' rapport with the daring Miss Holmes was lost almost overnight. A variety of reasons have been advanced over the years—a changing audience taste, ineffective independent distribution, a poor serial—but a combination of these factors seems most probable. At any rate, 1920 found Helen at the low point in her career, reduced to working for the near-bankrupt Warner Brothers in a jungle serial, *The Tiger Band,* and lending them operating capital (which she regained only after a lawsuit) in the process.

Throughout the twenties, Helen made a large number of inde-

Helen rescues Leo Maloney in A Lass of The Lumberlands.

pendent westerns (*Ghost City, Whispering Smith, Medicine Bend*)—writing in the railroad background whenever possible and sharing the billing with William Desmond, Bruce Gordon and Franklin Farnum—but she was never able to recapture the status of a top star. Her greatest popularity had come at a time when the accepted roles of man-woman, hero-heroine had been reversed. She had been the "hero" and her somewhat unfortunate and bumbling leading man (usually Leo Maloney) served mainly as a convenient object to be rescued by her cool daring. But after World War I, the roles reverted back to their accepted norm and Helen did little more than smile at the camera and execute an occasional stunt.

Directed for the most part by McGowan, Helen's feature appearances came in program pictures. The action was spread thickly across a slender plot line, relying so heavily on her love affair with the locomotive that it was sometimes difficult to distinguish between her films. She was now performing for an entire generation of movie-goers which had never seen her serials of a few years before, and thus remained quite unaware that this vivacious brunette had once faced death weekly at a time when stunt actresses were at a premium. The few dangerous feats Helen undertook in her features were mild in comparison, especially now that she was occasionally allowed the luxury of a double! But the competition was great; it almost seemed as if everyone in the business during the twenties was a stunt acrobat (or had a double who was) and the excitement of a horse-to-train transfer, which had once brought a hush over the audience, was now commonplace in Reel 3 and taken for granted by the thrill-satiated fans of mounted melodrama, mostly the small fry set.

As a result, Helen Holmes found herself just another working girl and the scramble back to the top in a make-believe world, where reputations and popularity had no meaning beyond the last picture in which she had worked, became a near-impossible accomplishment. While some personalities were typecast by their roles, others were similarly restricted by circumstances and Helen's forte, the western/railroad thriller, had been relegated to the Poverty Row producers and neighborhood theaters as the silent film entered its last decade. Working in the independent field, there was very little chance of her regaining any measure of the stardom she had once enjoyed, and

Helen and Leo Maloney (center) c. 1915, during a lunch break from filming of chapter of Hazards of Helen.

Taken from an original print, these frame enlargements from The Railroad Raiders *(1917) show the grit which brought Helen fame and fortune.*

another circumstance over which she had no control combined with this to frustrate her efforts.

Helen had been fortunate in earning a great deal of money, much of which she had wisely saved. Her marriage to McGowan had ended in divorce and she wed Lloyd Saunders, a stunt man

As a western railroad adventure heroine, Helen's features and serials contained exciting moments for adventure fans. Whether leaping from a moving car to speeding train. . . .

Or to a runaway buckboard, Helen gave the fans their money's worth. From Rayart's The Lost Express, *1926.*

and cowboy. Retiring from the screen in 1926, they moved to Sonora, investing their savings in a huge ranch, confident that there would be no financial worries for the rest of their lives. Seven consecutive drought years wiped them out and Saunders was forced to return to the rodeo circuit. Although Helen made two attempts to regain a foothold in front of the camera in the thirties, everyone in a position to give her work seemed to have a very short memory.

Helen eventually moved to the San Fernando Valley, where she occupied her time training dogs for the screen and running a small antique shop. Unlike so many former screen greats, Miss Holmes retained her dignity and perspective, refusing to berate an industry that had closed its doors on a near-charter member. A recurrence of tuberculosis complicated her last years and she was a youthful 58 years old when she passed away in 1950. Helen Holmes was content, however, in knowing that she had tasted the fruits of a world's adulation for a few short years before movie stardom became synonomous with press agentry.

★★★

Al Hoxie

Whenever Al Hoxie's westerns are mentioned, cinema historians and critics can be heard to mutter "absolute boredom," and not too long ago, when queried about the silent westerns in which he starred, Al himself chuckled that "they were all lousy." Rescreening a representative selection today, one almost has to agree with Hoxie's judgment; the majority of his films were shoddy in virtually every respect. Yet how to explain the surprising number of fans around the world who still remember some (or all) of the two dozen western features in which Al Hoxie starred between 1925–29? Many take the time and effort to write the aging cowpuncher (he was born in 1901 and just think of how many he has outlived!), expressing their admiration and discussing the fine points of a particular film which has remained vivid in their memory. Are they to be just dismissed for lack of taste or is there some perspective we have overlooked or perhaps forgotten in this sophisticated day of jet travel and space exploration? This residual of popularity after so many years indicates the strong impact the silent western made on its devotees.

Al Hoxie was a manifestation of the extreme interest in western action and adventure pictures which characterized the silent film during the twenties. True enough, his starring roles were related to the success of his brother Jack, but Al Hoxie was no slouch: he could shoot it out or scrap with the best of them and his pictures breathed mainly *Action*, exactly what the second- and third-run houses wanted. As in the case of the silent serials of the period, logic and coherent story line sometimes went completely out the window. But audiences continued to clamor for more of the same and independent showmen like Morris Schlank and William Pizor gave it to them in ample doses, creating an entirely new spectrum of lower-magnitude stars as they went along. Al Hoxie was one of those who caught the matinee public's fancy for a brief time and therein lay the key to his success—the audiences to whom his films played.

Even though it was brief, Alton Hoxie had a starring career which fans still remember.

Al visits brother Jack and his family—daughters Pearl, Ramona and wife Marin Sais.

Al doubled for his brother in many of Jack's early features.

Hoxie was no slouch with the women, but scenes like this one slowed down the pace of his pictures considerably.

The Road Agent

The independent western had much more in common with the serials of the twenties than just bad stories. As the decade wore along, audiences for these two entertainment formats became increasingly filled with children; the adults were deserting the screen for other forms of diversion. By the middle of the decade, many producers aimed their films almost entirely for the youngsters, and as such the requirements for story line and plot development were made less stringent by the substitution of fancy riding and hard fighting, as the good guy whipped the baddies every Saturday afternoon. The economics of producing this greatly simplified type of entertainment were undeniable and many producers built healthy bank accounts in just this manner.

How did Al do it? Born in Nez Perce, Idaho, on October 7, 1901 (an Indian reservation at the time), young Hoxie moved with his family to Riggins, a small town on the Salmon River in Idaho where he grew up and punched cattle on local ranches for a living until 1919, when wanderlust took him to California where brother Jack was about to hit it big in the picture business. Al's movie debut came with a small part as the brother of Marin Sais (soon to be Jack's wife in real life) in National Film's *Thunderbolt Jack*, a

15-episode western serial; and when Jack's ascending career took him to Arrow, Al went along to double his brother and play small roles. In the early twenties, his parts included the Indian chief in Arrow's *Days of '49,* a role in William S. Hart's final film, *Tumbleweed,* and the heavy in a number of the Fred Gilman westerns.

But Morris Schlank's Anchor Productions had signed a distribution contract with W. Ray Johnston's Rayart Productions and the producer was looking for a western star to go along with the series of Helen Holmes western railroad features he was filming. Al Hoxie possessed the necessary qualifications—he was tall, rugged and rather handsome, with a bashful but infectious grin that slowly spread from ear to ear. In addition, he was also available—an important consideration in an era when all of the established names were hard at work grinding out westerns on an assembly line basis which rivaled the production of a sausage factory. The fact that Al looked a good deal like his more famous brother didn't hurt, nor did his name. *Voila!*—raised from the ranks to stardom, of a sort.

One of Al's films for Schlank, *The Ace of Clubs,* stands out as the probable low point in the history of the silent western—it was so unbelievably bad that today's viewer finds it hard to decide

Hoxie's best friend was his horse, Pardner.

Al Hoxie with Jane Reed in Roaring Guns, *1928.*

whether to laugh or cry. Midway in the film, a sneaking suspicion arises that it was all one big hoax—a giant put-on—as the badly miscast actors played their roles with a combination of 1925 comedy and 1890 melodrama, coming across on-screen more like cartoon caricatures. Fortunately for Al, the script didn't require his appearance until the film was nearly half over, and about all the acting it called for was a wistful stare and heavy breathing at appropriate times—combined with a bit of hard riding, one stunt and three short fist fights.

His five-reelers were literally slapped together, requiring no more than eight days apiece to film, and Hoxie's three starring

Blue Streak O'Neill.

series were made for Anchor in 1925–26, Bud Barsky's Wild West Pictures in 1926–27 and Krelbar Picture Corporation in 1927–28. While under contract, Al earned $150 weekly but a few of his pictures brought him a flat fee of $500. This gives the reader some idea of the incredibly low cost of production involved in the independent westerns of the twenties and watching films like *The Ace of Clubs*, *Red Blood* and *The Texas Terror* shows the correlation between production costs and quality along Poverty Row during this period. Yet the Al Hoxie westerns made money for their producers and the star gained a following of youthful admirers who have helped keep his name alive in the gallery of silent sagebrush heroes. Between leading roles, Al kept busy with featured parts in the independent westerns of Art Acord and others until sound fastened its grip on the industry in 1929.

Drifting out of the movies about this time, Al entered the California State Forestry Service for awhile, then became a law enforcement officer for the city of Anaheim, ending his working career as chief security officer at Patton State Hospital in San Bernardino. Only two weeks before his retirement in 1968, Al was involved in a real-life situation reminiscent of his celluloid thrillers. Displaying the same cool courage which many of his film scripts called for, he quietly disarmed a berserk mental patient who had just shot two people. His retirement was accompanied by a nomination for the California State Medal of Honor, a fitting close to the career of Al Hoxie.

Jack Hoxie

(HE RIDES LIKE A CENTAUR; HE LOVES LIKE A ROMEO!)

Motion pictures were still just a vision in the eyes of a few men in January 1885 when Jack Hart Hoxie was born in a small cabin on Kingfish Creek near Guthrie, Oklahoma. Yet Hoxie was destined to become one of the more popular heroes of the silent western. Although he never pretended to be much of an actor (and he wasn't), Jack was a true *Son of the West* and his films usually emphasized his prowess with horse, rope and gun.

After a childhood somewhat comparable to an American version of a Charles Dickens novel, Hoxie joined the Dick Stanley Wild West Show as a bronc rider and bulldogger. In spite of the keen competition, Jack soon became its top attraction and when the show's owner was killed during a tour of the West Coast in 1912, Hoxie took over as manager to complete the obligated appearances before closing the show. The end of this tour left him in California, and overnight bronc-busting Jack Hoxie became Hartford Hoxie, fledgling motion picture actor. Working as an extra, bit player, double—any role that came along—Hoxie became an oft-used Universal contract player in the next five years, with roles ranging from brief appearance in *The Dumb Girl of Portici* and Geraldine Farrar's *Joan the Woman* to supporting parts in a number of Hobart Bosworth's pictures. When the Universal lot had nothing for him to do, Jack freelanced and can be seen in walk-on roles in several chapters of Kalem's railroad series, *The Hazards of Helen*.

But real stardom eluded Hoxie until 1919, when "Smiling Billy" Parsons of the National Film Corporation signed Jack for the lead role in *Lightning Bryce,* co-starring Ann Little. For an independent serial, *Lightning Bryce* was rather well done and Jack appeared the following year with Marin Sais (his female lead, whom he married the following year) in *Thunderbolt Jack,* another National serial

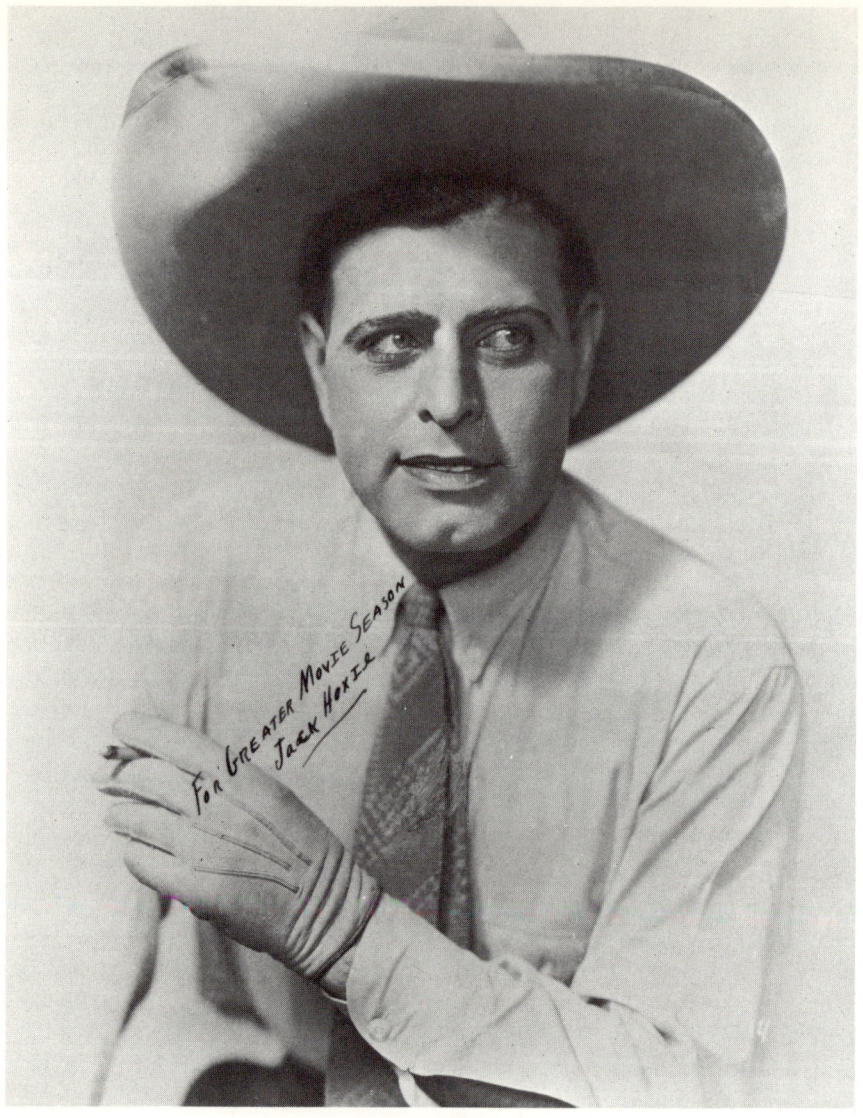

Jack Hoxie.

and one which western fans now regard as something of a benchmark in the history of cactus chapter plays—it launched Jack Hoxie on a lengthy starring career.

A magnificent physical speciman of the stereotype western hero, six-foot Jack Hoxie towered over the bad men, symbolic of the eternal dominance of good over evil to his young fans. On-screen, he projected the image of the rugged, admirable and honest man who always defeated villainy—and Saturday matinee audiences loved him for it. Off-screen, Jack enjoyed nothing better than a good drink and a rousing poker game, but his public never knew

Jack, his family and brother Al.

Marin Sais frees Jack from behind bars . . .

And our hero returns the favor.

that their hero was anything other than he appeared to be in his pictures. With a meticulous pride in his image, Hoxie felt he owed that much to his small fans.

Jack's two serials for National Film did so well at the box-office that when Parsons decided to film a Tarzan serial, he announced that Jack would play the leading role as the modern incarnation of the Edgar Rice Burroughs ape man. But Hoxie felt he deserved more money, and when Parsons balked at an increase in salary Jack threatened a court action restraining the use of his name in connection with the Tarzan role. He signed instead with Ben Wilson's

Unity Photoplays (which released through Arrow, the distributor of Jack's two National serials) and, co-starring with Marin Sais, made two series of feature westerns (*Dead or Alive, Devil Dog Dawson, Barb Wire*) which were strong on action with little attention paid to the romantic element. These led to still another independent series, this time for Anthony J. Xydias's Sunset Productions in 1922. Directed mainly by Robert North Bradbury, whose proficiency at grinding out films during the twenties was exceeded only by that of J. P. McGowan, they were not particularly good films,[1] but Jack managed to land a berth at Universal in 1923, where he spent his best years.

Universal was the largest producer of western short subjects and features after World War I, and with Hoot Gibson, Harry

Jack and Marin Sais in a scene from **Thunderbolt Jack,** *his National serial of 1920 which launched his starring career in features.*

---

[1] The reviewer for *The Motion Picture News* suggested that only Hoxie's acting kept the first of the series, *Barb Wire,* from being a total disaster. As Hoxie was no actor, it must have been a really sad affair.

While Hoxie sometimes worked with a posse . . .

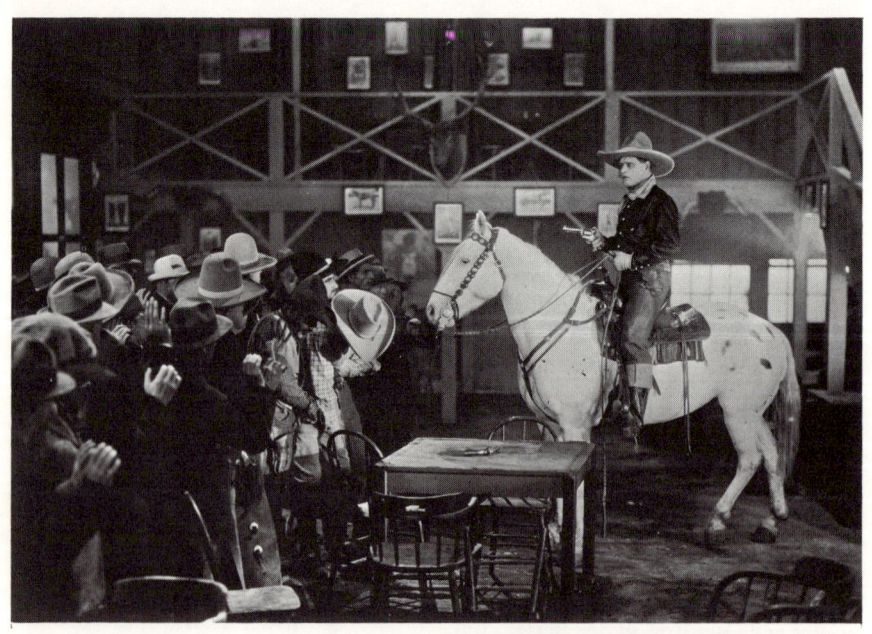

. . . . .He really preferred his heroic moments alone.

Hoxie cut a dashing figure as long as he wasn't acting or making love.

Jack demonstrates his roping skill for wife Marin Sais, who took a break from filming to try out their new Lexington Lark.

White Fury, Josephine Hill, Jack and Joe Bonomo in Heroes of the Wild, *Jack's Mascot serial of 1927.*

Carey, William Desmond and Art Acord riding the Universal range, along with many others of lesser stature, Jack's talents and personality were soon absorbed into its assembly-line approach to production. For several years, Hoxie ranked close behind Hoot Gibson as Universal's second most popular cowpoke and his films were accorded the same treatment as those of Hoot; they were released in alternation with the features made by Gibson and Desmond. This most peculiar circumstance was regarded by the Universal executives as offering audiences a change of pace, as Jack was the opposite of both in nearly every respect.

Although a bit of a ham, Hoxie's acting left much to be desired, and while the party responsible for the innumerable close-ups in his films probably went unpunished, he should have suffered some strange malady for his perverted sense of humor. In anything but

Josephine Hill and Jack have located the treasure, but how will they escape from this dire peril? From Heroes of the Wild.

a close-up, the camera was kind to Jack, emphasizing the virile appearance expected of a western star. Of course, as Jack put on weight in the latter twenties, the camera was not quite so flattering to him, but when Hoxie faced the lens at close range—with his face tightened up in what must kindly be described as grim determination—the entire effect quickly dissipated, especially in a romantic clinch. Yet, even with stock stories and fair to indifferent direction, Jack Hoxie went on to become a Saturday afternoon institution in the mid-twenties.

His better films were made in 1925–26 (*Wild Horse Stampede, The Fighting Peacemaker, Red Hot Leather, The White Outlaw*) under the direction of Cliff Smith and Al Rogell, who kept their hero a respectable distance from the camera as much as possible. Along with the westerns of Tom Mix, Hoxie's films were com-

Hoxie's favorite role was that of Buffalo Bill in The Last Frontier. *On the right, a youthful Bill Boyd—Hopalong Cassidy to a later generation.*

Hampered by his lack of sufficient formal education, Jack's career in talkies was restricted to the cheapest of independent westerns and forced his retirement from the screen.

mendable for the colorful location scenery, and fortunately efforts to inject a comic note by the star were held to a minimum. As an actor Jack was bad enough; as a comedian or romantic lead, he was totally at sea—regardless of Universal's billing. But put Hoxie in the saddle where he was at home and turn him loose! Now it was a different ball game—the kids clapped until their sweaty palms ached. The more riding and fighting that could be crammed into five reels the less time for acting, and Rogell kept his star in the saddle as much as possible. Like many of his contemporaries, Jack's constant and most trusted companion for a time was his dog, Bunk.

By 1928, the program western was in deep trouble and so was Jack's career. His popularity had slowly begun to fade, and in the fall of 1927, he had returned to the chapter play to boost a sagging public interest. *Heroes of the Wild* was a rousing Mascot cliff hanger, but it did little to restore Hoxie's slipping box-office appeal—a problem faced by many of his celluloid cow pals as they watched the western suffer a decline in favor. When it surfaced to an even larger audience in the early thirties, their ranks would be swollen by many new and younger faces eager to take their boots and saddles. Jack was one who lost his.

Although he starred in numerous talkies, Hoxie's lack of elocution and acting ability combined to restrict him to the cheapest of independent films and Jack finished his career touring the country with various Wild West Shows. Years later, Jack Hoxie would point with pride to but one role; in 1926, he had been personally chosen by Cecil B. DeMille to play Buffalo Bill in *The Last Frontier*. The honor of this selection somehow made it all worth while to the once-popular cowboy star and remained the high point of a career which, spanning nearly four decades in front of the camera, had brought worldwide fame and fortune to the kid from Kingfish Creek.

Fred Humes

Fred Humes? Who was Fred Humes? If this question passed through your mind when you came to this section, don't feel badly about it; there's a good chance that you're not the only one wondering who he was and why he's featured here. Fred was one of those screen cowpokes whose producers could never decide with any degree of certainty just where he belonged, or why, and so Humes's career alternated between short subjects and features, supporting parts and starring roles with all the regularity and monotony of a yo-yo in action.

A Dubois, Pennsylvania, boy whose pre-screen career also had its ups and downs, Fred spent several years in secondary roles before graduating to leading parts in a series of Universal western short subjects in 1925 (*Taking Chances, Gold Trap, Man with the Scar*). By the next year, Humes was busily scurrying from set to set with leading roles in both the two-reel Universal Mustangs (*The Call of Hazard, Frame Up, Trapped*) and the five-reel Blue Streak series (*Yellow Back, Range Courage, Broncho Buster*).

His career never exactly set the world on fire, and when sound struck the industry Humes was quickly lost in the ensuing shuffle. But he did make a number of low-budget westerns with a definite slant toward comedy between 1925 and 1928 which, although forgotten today along with their star, held a certain interest at the time, and one which devoted western fans still retain. The epitome of the tried-and-true formula western, his Universal films deviated very little from the established pattern. The Mustang short subjects constituted a training program for potential stars like Fred and directors hopefully on their way up, like William Wyler, William Crinley and Edgar Lewis. While not outstanding in any respect, they were usually constructed around a tightly-woven but easily followed plot which had been reworked so many times by the Universal writing staff that the formula was firmly fixed in everyone's mind. Program pictures in the truest sense of the assembly line, the direction was fairly smooth and the photography uniform.

Fred Humes.

Within this unobjectionable framework, one found the usual share of hard riding and snappy fighting by Humes, who tried his level best to rise above the crowd, only to find his feet firmly nailed to the floor, partially as a result of his own limitations as a heroic type and partially because of the bland mixture that these formula films spilled onto the screen. As an actor Fred was adequate, although at times he gave every appearance of an actor imitating a non-actor. A modest man who put everything he had into each new role, Fred kept busy in front of the grinding cameras, yet nothing

Ena Gregory, Fred Humes in **Blazing Days**.

more than his weekly paycheck rewarded even his best efforts. With new western stars arriving on the screen like spring flowers during this period, it must have been discouraging to Humes to work so hard and accomplish so little, but the undefinable chemistry of stardom was simply not there.

1928 arrived and Fred was still at it. Only the name had been changed—now he was starring in the Ranch Rider series. Universal's Blue Streak westerns were finished, replaced by what the firm chose to call its "Adventure" series. With *The Fearless Rider, Put 'Em Up* and others under his belt, Humes's career as a leading man was at its peak, but the long fall to obscurity was close at hand.

Fred had the misfortune to arrive in features at a time when the competition was quite stiff and the western was beginning to feel both the pressures of a slowly dying market and the uncertainties with which the distant rumblings of synchronized sound complicated the future. He further suffered from the formula picture and a lack of the distinct characterization called box-office appeal. Yet, modest programmers that they were, his features did have their entertaining moments and did not suffer from comparison to many of the westerns released by Sierra, Rayart and other independents. Like Ted Wells and Newton House, who rode beside

Fred has it in for Charles Quinn in The Broncho Buster *as Dave Dunbar looks on.*

Humes takes a moment out while filming Range Courage.

Put 'Em Up

Fred and Barbara Worth in The Fearless Riders

Broncho Buster.

him on the Universal range, Fred's future never held forth any real promise—he was the victim of circumstances and a system over which he had no real control. Had Fred Humes made it to leading roles earlier in the twenties, he just might have had an even chance, or would he?

Al Jennings

(THE BANDIT KING OF THE SCREEN)

If any man were qualified to appear on the western screen by virtue of an appropriate past career, that man would have to be Al Jennings of Oklahoma. Of all the celluloid heroes, his infamous real-life career as cowboy lawyer, train robber, convict and general all-around badman was matched only by Tom Mix, whose pre-screen background had been equally illustrious but on the side of law and order. Born and raised in Virginia, Alphonso J. Jennings had been one of the last of the famous western outlaws and after being pardoned by President Theodore Roosevelt in 1907 (after serving only five years of a life sentence), the reformed heavy trod the straight and narrow. It wasn't nearly so interesting, exciting or challenging as the life he had given up, but in the process Al discovered that there were a lot of people in the world foolish enough to pay good money just to listen to him recite spine-tingling incidents from his past, spiced with periodic affirmations that he had indeed learned his lesson.

And Al had some rip-snorting tales to tell! After the Jennings gang had bungled an attempt to blow open a baggage car safe (the car was destroyed; the safe stood intact), Al had concluded that no self-respecting bandit worthy of the name would leave the scene of a crime empty-handed, so he robbed the passengers of their jewelry and about $400 in cash, salvaging a bunch of bananas and a two-gallon jug of whisky from the wrecked car before riding away. Stories such as this earned the ex-bandit a reputation for his sense of humor, and Al was publicly acknowledged by that master story teller, O. Henry, as the source of some of his short stories; the two had served time together in Ohio State Penitentiary.

Before embarking on his life of crime, Al had practiced law in Coldwater, Kansas, and then moved to El Reno, Oklahoma Territory,

Al Jennings.

where a feud with local politicians eventually cost him his career. Once his citizenship had been restored by the pardon, Al picked up his law career, and in 1912 he ran for public office in Oklahoma (he sought the Oklahoma County Attorney's seat), losing by such a small vote that many Oklahomans were convinced he had been cheated by the political machine.

A frame enlargement of Al in action from **The Lady of the Dugout.**

When the Thanhouser Film Company offered him $5000 to use the story he had co-authored for the *Saturday Evening Post* in 1913 as the basis of a film depicting his life and hired him as its technical advisor, Al discovered that the profitable veins he had been mining on the lecture circuit had a Mother Lode—the movies. But encouraged by his fine showing at the polls in 1912, Al succumbed to political fever and entered the 1914 Democratic primary in Oklahoma, seeking nomination to the Governor's post. Not surprisingly, he polled but 21,732 votes, coming in third. When he had run for the county attorney's post, Oklahoma politicians had laughed, but this time they made every effort to point out to the voters that an ex-jailbird in the Governor's chair would make the state the laughing stock of the Union.

And so Al turned his attention back to his favorite topic, "Crime Does Not Pay." His entrance into the land of easy money was thus delayed until after World War I, but by 1919 Al had given movies a whirl with an appearance in one of Vitagraph's *Wolfville Tales*. Finding the world of make-believe to be a most agreeable one, Al set up his own production company and arranged for distribution

Al was close to 50 when he came to the screen in heroic roles, and every year of his age shows in this clip from The Lady of the Dugout.

Al and James Cagney on location for The Oklahoma Kid, *1939. Al often served as a historical or technical advisor during his later years.*

Whether playing outlaw or lawman, Al's screen character exhibited a gallant attitude toward females.

through the Capital Film Company, but made most of his films on location in Arizona instead of California.

While giving his reputation as a reformed bandit a big play for publicity purposes, Jennings often stepped across the imaginary line to portray a law enforcement officer on-screen, enjoying every minute of the irony. As a western hero, Al violated every precept in the book. Short and thin, almost anemic in appearance, his craggy face lined by 46 years and accentuated by a shock of unruly auburn hair, he could only be described as a homely professional ex-bandit play-acting for the camera. His stiff manner on the screen was exactly as in real life; discerning audiences thought that he walked through his paces as smoothly as a ten-year old in a Sunday school play, but to the youngsters who quickly became his most avid fans, this one-time law-breaker was as real as life itself, and so Al Jennings rode a thin beam of light in a darkened theatre with a good deal more success than he had enjoyed in the days when he rode a galloping horse, chasing the gold-filled baggage car at the end of the outlaw's rainbow.

Ham actor that he was, one had to give Al credit for one thing; his two-reel western stories were actually miniature morality plays, both in tone and viewpoint. In films like *The Fugitive's Life, Lost in Society* and *Fate's Mockery,* Jennings did his best to emphasize the rewards of righteousness, not for himself as much as for those with whom he came in contact. *The Tryout* was a good example and one in which he portrayed the good-badman, a concept of the western outlaw developed by Broncho Billy Anderson and perfected by William S. Hart.

As the outlaw leader in *The Tryout,* Al tolerated no nonsense, quickly establishing his basic good character by befriending Vivian Gane and her child, whose husband was a "shiftless skunk," as the subtitles informed us. Threatening the drunken husband with dire consequences if he did not mend his ways, Al rode off into the sunset—a lonely bandit whose way of life was devoid of romance and similar niceties. Riding hard to catch up with Jennings and his gang, the son indicated his desire to become a fearless outlaw leader like Al, his hero. Instead of turning the boy away, Al decided to let him ride with the band as a lesson, forcing the responsibilities of manhood upon his youthful recruit; and before the second reel had ended, the boy's basic decency had been reestablished. Bad man that he was, Al Jennings had prevented the straying of another soul from the path of honesty and virtue.

But the market for independent short subjects and western features of the variety Al was peddling became saturated in the early twenties and the unexpected collapse of Capital cost him a considerable sum in the form of anticipated revenues. As a result, Al was soon forced to close his Al Jennings Feature Film Company in Culver City. For awhile, the former renegade turned up occassionally with small roles in westerns, but he soon faded from the screen almost as quietly as he had appeared.

In 1951, Al was briefly restored to public life by Dan Duryea's sympathetic portrayal in "Al Jennings of Oklahoma," a fairly factual biopic, but Jennings soon slipped back into the obscurity of his memento-crowded home in Tarzana, California, where his sharp wit and engrossing tall tales captivated visitors and neighbors alike until his death at age 98 in 1962.

Buck Jones

While stars were often noted for their temperament, producers were also known for certain devious tricks, one of which was to hire an unknown and, giving him the full treatment, create a new star whose very presence on the lot served to keep the other and more valuable property in line. Although this was done with some regularity in the early days, it was seldom that such a disciplinary maneuver actually produced another star of any magnitude. More often than not, this technique was used on the whim of some offended front-office executive, but the implication was not lost on the errant star and once he stepped back into the producer's good graces, the newcomer was suddenly forgotten or just allowed to coast along as best he could. Charles Gebhart was a rare example of successful "captive competition"; his popularity was to eventually rival that of the man for whose boots and saddle he had been groomed.

As Buck Jones, Gebhart brought to the screen a background which included military service with the Sixth U.S. Cavalry in the Philippines, the Indianapolis Speedway, Miller Brothers 101 Ranch Wild West Show and the Ringling Brothers Circus. While on tour in Los Angeles, Buck left the circus for the movies, making his debut as a sheepherder in one of Universal's numerous western short subjects, but World War I interrupted his career as an extra and double, sending him to the battlefields of France. After the war, Buck returned to Hollywood, signing a contract with Canyon Pictures to support Franklyn Farnum in his series of two-reelers. In a few of these films, Buck appeared on-screen as much as Farnum and had ample opportunity to display his talents.

Meanwhile, William Fox was having problems with his star western attraction, Tom Mix. On the threat of quitting the picture business, Tom was demanding a substantial salary increase. Looking around for a replacement should this catastrophe come to pass, Fox executives settled on Buck Jones as the lever they needed to hold

Buck Jones.

Mix in place. His Canyon contract completed, Jones had joined the Fox payroll as a $40.00 a week stuntman. This was increased to $150, and Buck received his chance at stardom in *The Last Straw*, a Fox release of early 1920.

An immediate hit with exhibitors and fans, Buck Jones went on to make 61 more western features in his eight years with Fox. Backing him up with solid writing from the pens of Jackson Gregory and Fred Jackman, and expert direction by W. S. Van Dyke and Scott Dunlap, Fox soon had its second western star attraction at the box-office in the person of Buck Jones. Jones's films bore a faint resemblance to the earlier westerns of the now-fading

William S. Hart, for while the scripts called for action and lots of it in place of plot and realism, Buck's rugged he-man appearance, low-key acting and realistic western dress tended to offset the flamboyant format which Tom Mix had ridden to fame. Some of his later westerns for Fox were rather light-hearted affairs, with Buck handling the comedy himself instead of relying upon the comic sidekick so prevalent in westerns of the twenties.

While challenging Tom Mix for the distinction of top Fox attraction in the twenties, Buck Jones's salary had risen to $3500 weekly; and not unlike Mix, Buck had ambitions which went beyond Fox. One was his own production company, and by 1928 he had accumulated enough money to leave Fox and begin the first of his BUCK JONES PRODUCTIONS, *The Big Hop*. Unfortunately, Jones had picked the wrong time to become an independent, as the novelty of sound had caught on just as the film was completed. Using the Cortella Phone System, synchronized music and sound effects on discs were hurriedly added to the silent feature and *The Big Hop* went into states-right distribution. With its story of the western rancher involved in a trans-Pacific flying contest, the sage-

Buck and Winifred Westover in Firebrand Trevision.

When it came to extracting information, Buck was a pretty lenient fellow, if he got the information he wanted...

But a refusal to talk brought strong action.

Jones was not afraid to take on an entire gang if necessary, as in this scene from Sunset Sprague.

"If you don't pay attention, you'll never learn how to blow this safe." Eileen Percy was Buck's pupil in Pardon My Nerve, *1922.*

The Fast Mail.

brush hero was out of his element, and this time his usually good reviews had soured—Buck Jones lost $50,000 and abandoned his film company to turn to another of his ambitions, THE BUCK JONES WILD WEST SHOW.

During the height of his popularity at Fox, the Buck Jones Rangers had been organized across the country as a promotional stunt, and at one time numbered some four million of his young fans. Over the years, Buck had seriously considered the idea of returning to the outdoor western show, putting together his own and taking it around the country to cities and towns where large numbers of his Rangers could be counted on to swell the attendance figures. A fine idea, but after only one month on the road, Buck was forced to close the show down. A victim of the Depression and unwise business management, he was $300,000 poorer for the experience.

By this time, the silent western had faded away; sound had completely taken over the range and in order to get Buck back into the screen saddle, Scott Dunlap, now his manager, was forced to sign Jones with Sol Lesser's Beverly Pictures at $300 weekly, quite a comedown for the one-time Fox star. But before long, Buck regained both his financial standing and his fans, appearing on the

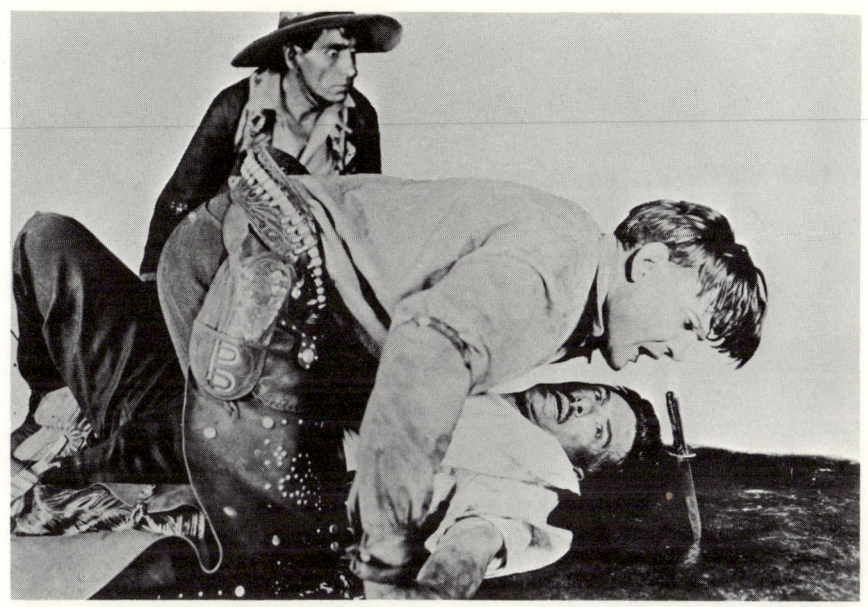

Buck's films were filled with good clean action, enjoyed by all his youthful fans, as shown by this attempted knifing from Sunset Sprague.

Francis Lee and Buck in "Good As Gold", 1927.

Buck and Silver rode their way through many westerns together.

The advent of sound did not stop Buck Jones; he was a popular favorite until his tragic death in the Cocoanut Grove holocaust.

The famous Jones profile during a relaxed moment away from the movie camera.

screen for the next twelve years under the Columbia, Universal and Monogram banners in a large number of westerns, some good and some bad, but few recapturing the high quality of his silent pictures.

On the evening of November 28, 1942, Buck Jones attended a party at the Coconut Grove in Boston, hosted in his honor by a group of New England exhibitors. Over 300 persons died in the tragic conflagration which swept the famed dinner club that night; one was 53-year-old Buck Jones, who died while helping others to safety. Thus he became in real life what he had been on the screen—a hero.

J. Warren Kerrigan

Because of their continuing character, the Essanay films of Broncho Billy Anderson are the ones best remembered for their pioneering contributions to the western genre, but none of the early producers did more to popularize this form of entertainment than the American Film Manufacturing Company with its "Flying A" westerns starring J. Warren Kerrigan. Jack Kerrigan's career was not primarily that of a western star, but the circumstances surrounding his early years in front of a camera found him starring in as many as 100 short westerns annually and his career was climaxed by the leading role in James Cruze's classic, *The Covered Wagon*. In between this beginning and end, he had made many other pictures of a non-western nature, none of which are especially memorable today.

Before entering the movies, Kerrigan's stage experience had been rather limited; his greatest fame was reflected in a nickname, "The Gibson Man." An unusually handsome chap and the fashion plate of his day, Jack was best known as a male model; the nickname reflected his position as the masculine counterpart of Charles Dana Gibson's famed "Gibson Girl." Neither modeling nor the stage offered the security of a regular pay check and so Kerrigan joined Essanay's Chicago studio in early 1910, first appearing on-screen in *A Voice From the Fireplace*. Jack encountered little difficulty in acquiring the rudiments of motion picture acting and when Samuel S. Hutchison formed the American brand in October 1910, J. Warren Kerrigan was the first actor hired.

Hutchison sent the new company West to make pictures beyond the watchful eye of the Motion Picture Patents Company, which frowned upon competition from outside its select circle. Settling at Santa Barbara, California, the American company set to work and Kerrigan started his rapid rise to fame. Before long, the "Flying A" trademark was seen in theatres across the country, and for many months Jack Kerrigan played the lead in nearly every American release to so grace the screen.

J. Warren Kerrigan

American concentrated on westerns at first; they were easy to film using the natural scenery and thus required little investment in expensive sets. As its sole star, Jack found several things working in his favor. Unlike Broncho Billy and others who rode the early screen range, his handsome boyish features were quite photogenic and Jack was fairly good at playing light comedy, both assets in attracting a female following. The scripts for his films were solidly

For over a year, Jack starred in virtually every Flying A release, adding a dimension to the western beyond that portrayed by Broncho Billy. This scene is from Eastern Flower, *1913*.

written dramas with comic values; their theme usually required Jack to use his brain rather than brawn in overcoming adversity, a fortunate circumstance in view of his slight build.

The "Flying A" westerns did not follow the stylized and sterile format typical of much of their competition (which would soon become the most outstanding characteristic of the western); they were authentic slices of life in a western setting, put on the screen at a time when early moviegoers were tiring of the surfeit of artificial westerns. Their clarity of expression was very similar in nature to the westerns Tom Ince was making for Kessel and Bauman's Bison release—an attribute lacking in the Broncho Billy films. Even so, Kerrigan's films were not perfect; many found him playing a Mexican role and identified as "Tony," but pictures such as *The Poisoned Flume* and *Truth in the Wilderness* were far ahead of most westerns of the 1912–13 period.

In less than two years on the screen, American's westerns had placed the company on a very sound financial footing and Jack Kerrigan reached the pinnacle of stardom, placing third in the 1913 *Motion Picture Story Magazine*'s popularity poll. Strangely enough, Kerrigan's acting was not really all that good, but his good looks

Jack (r) was also seen in American's Calamity Anne *series, which starred Louise Lester. Here they are in* Calamity Anne, Detective, *1913.*

Kerrigan often played a Mexican identified to audiences by subtitles as "Tony."

and personable manner had combined to give him the distinct advantage of becoming the western's first matinee idol. Almost alone, he had boosted the "Flying A" brand into a position of prominence, but now it was clear enough to Jack that American could do nothing further to help the career of J. Warren Kerrigan.

Enter Carl Laemmle, president of Universal and Hollywood's version of the western claim jumper. Laying in wait for the unsuspecting producer who had created a star property, Laemmle was noted for spiriting the actor or actress away in the dead of night with an offer too attractive to refuse. The recipient of such a proposition, Jack mounted his horse and headed south, moving his boots and saddle to Universal's lot where his own unit set to work filming westerns.

Production values of his Universal pictures took a curious turn —casts were larger and characterizations better defined, but story lines reflected the assembly-line production prevalent at Universal. Nonetheless, Kerrigan's popularity continued and he played non-western leads as well, even appearing as Samson in a film of the same name. By 1917, he had formed his own company and released his pictures through Paralta.

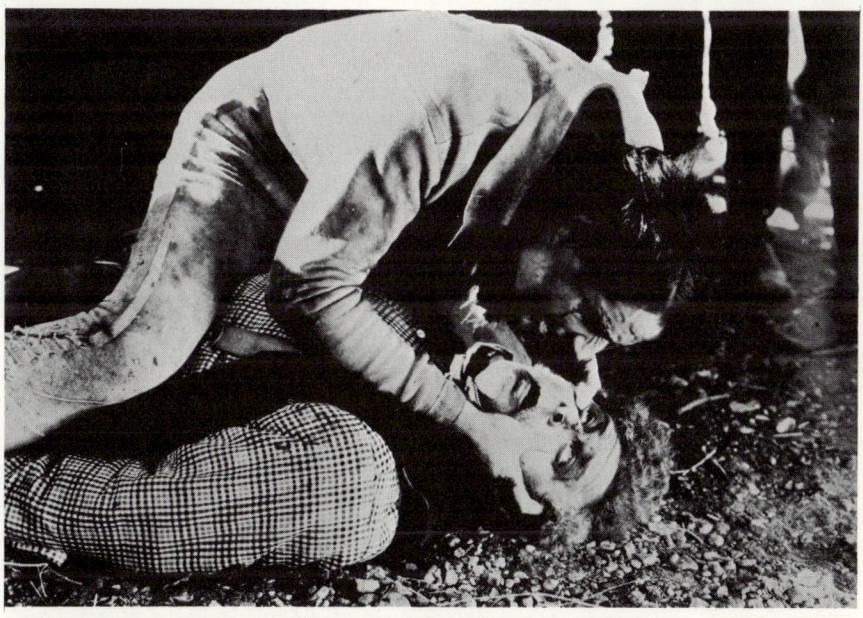

Jack's best-remembered role was in Paramount's 1923 epic western, **The Covered Wagon.** *In a vicious fight, he attempted to gorge Alan Hale's eyes out.*

The panoramic sweep of The Covered Wagon *and its pioneer trek to Oregon captivated western fans.*

Jack's career was virtually shattered by World War I. At a time when patriotic fever was running high, many stars voluntarily left the screen to serve in uniform. Kerrigan steadfastly refused to do so and the public wanted to know why. Jack's reasons were his own; he was 34, but because of his extremely youthful appearance on-screen, no amount of explanation on the part of the star, his producers or friends could convince the world at large that Jack Kerrigan was not a coward, hiding behind the status of movie stardom when his country needed him the most.

By 1920, J. Warren Kerrigan was nearly a completely forgotten man. Occasionally a role or two would come his way in one of the lesser independent pictures hoping to cash in on the former star value of an actor who would now work quite cheaply, but for all practical purposes Jack was living in an enforced retirement when the leading role in Paramount's screen adaptation of Emerson Hough's novel, *The Covered Wagon* came his way in 1922. Originally purchased as a vehicle for Mary Miles Minter, her refusal to endure the location shooting led Paramount to cast it as an "all-star" production (meaning no stars) and Jack saddled up to ride the comeback trail at a time when the western had suffered a major decline in audience interest.

The Indian attack sequence in The Covered Wagon *was masterfully staged under a foreboding sky.*

A somewhat pedestrian story of the pioneers' trek to Oregon, *The Covered Wagon* was a huge success with the public, rekindling interest in the genre and catapulting Kerrigan into the limelight once again. Audiences were captivated by the portrayal of the pioneers' hardships, including Indian attacks, fires and raging streams to cross, even though William S. Hart stood ready to point out that historically the picture contained many flaws. Fortunately, director James Cruze was able to capture the spirit of the journey in a stark, almost documentary fashion and this larger theme overshadowed the shallow plot line in what has now come to be regarded by critics as the first of the epic westerns.

Basking in the public acclaim that had rejuvenated a stagnant career, Jack starred in a few more films and then invested his savings in an extravagant production of *Captain Blood* for Vitagraph release, planning to use his recent success to permanently recapture the status of major stardom. Sadly, *Captain Blood* turned out to be a dreadful bore to critics and bombed at the box-office, closing the book on the starring career of 40-year-old J. Warren Kerrigan, who, with G. M. Anderson, had rescued the early western from oblivion.

★★★

Leo Maloney

Independent westerns of the twenties suffered from a lack of money to buy the talent necessary to turn out films with the dash and polish of the Mix or Hoot Gibson pictures, but it is quite likely that even had the money been available to them, few producers would have spent it. The maximum earning potential of "B" westerns was pretty well established by the state-right distribution system and the lower the cost at which a series could be brought in, the greater the profit to its producer. Not enjoying the luxury of a national exchange system, the independent knew that a hit picture would bring little more than any other and so production along Poverty Row was pretty much a "fast-buck" proposition, with most of the independent producers subscribing to the theory of "quick and dirty" program pictures.

Not so Leo Maloney, who wrote, directed, produced and starred for nearly a decade in western shorts and features. Possessing a sense of personal pride and integrity not often found in the independent ranks, Maloney also had an in-depth background in the movie business that many other independent producers lacked. After attending Santa Clara College near his native San Jose and then working on local ranches for awhile, Leo had drifted into the movies around 1912, where he spent several years in the ranks making all kinds of pictures. Maloney finally achieved a modest degree of fame as a male lead to Helen Holmes in her *The Hazards of Helen* series at Kalem and when Miss Holmes went into the serial business with her own company, Maloney left Kalem to continue his leading roles opposite the fearless serial heroine.

The exposure gained in these Signal serials soon made him an audience favorite, and by the early twenties Leo's bankroll matched his business acumen. Selling Pathé on a series of western short subjects to be produced by himself and Ford Beebe, he assembled a supporting cast of familiar names (Pauline Curley, Whitehorse, Bud Osborne) and turned out both the *Santa Fe Mac* and *Range*

Leo Maloney, his horse Senator and dog Bullet.

Rider series, dramatic shorts liberally sprinkled with comedy and a human touch lacking in many competitive subjects of the period. Although he was 5′ 11″, Maloney's 170 pounds gave him a heavy-set appearance and his tendency to overact in the dramatic scenes (which were not edited tightly enough) was the one disturbing flaw in these enjoyable and profitable series.

Continuing their association, Maloney and Beebe moved into feature production for William Steiner release and the resulting films proved to be representative of the best independent westerns of the twenties. The stories were carefully sketched to produce a hero who was human; Maloney usually portrayed a lawman torn between a sense of duty and love for a girl. Unlike the stalwart sagebrush heroes who never succumbed to any distractions from duty, Leo could be and often was tempted by the female, who temporarily had her own way. This laid the basis for the remainder of the film, as Leo sought to restore his honor, winning over the misguided heroine in the process.

His constant companion was a dog named Bullet whose role was often pivotal to the plot. Had Bullet been half as smart as Rin-Tin-Tin, Maloney's westerns could never have lasted beyond the middle of Reel #1, but being something of a slow-witted canine, he would discover, investigate and then ignore a clue at an early

Leo received his first taste of fame working with Helen Holmes and J. P. McGowan (standing) in Kalem's The Hazards of Helen *and Helen's later Signal serials. Jauntily perched on the back of Helen's roadster, he's shown here on location around 1915.*

Leo in a dramatic moment from The Outlaw Express.

Unlike other western stars, Maloney favored the long coat and string tie in many of his westerns.

Leo Maloney and Aileen Ray, as they appeared in "Overland Bound", the first independent talking western and Leo's last picture.

Luck and Sand

stage in the picture. This tipped off the audience that the necessary evidence could be provided when needed in the final reel. Bullet was also prominently featured whenever a dangerous stunt was required; if you have never seen a dog jump from a 50-foot cliff onto the back of a galloping horseman, you have missed something in the way of delightful oddities.

Keeping his stable of supporting actors from the Range Rider series, Maloney added Josephine Hill and Leonard Clapham to the roster. Clapham, better known to talkie fans as Tom London, provided just the right touch of shiftless villainy to counter the dash and ginger which Maloney brought to his role. Leo balanced his strong stories (*A Perfect Alibi, The Loser's End* and *The Ridin' Fool*) with enough light comedy to relieve the melodrama and each one was edited in much the same way as Hoot Gibson's Universal oaters; a slow beginning to set the scene properly, with momentum building up through each reel to a hard riding, slug-fest windup at the finish.

Leo's "Maloford" westerns for Pathé in 1927–28 were even stronger in story and action; the ingeniously conceived plots of pictures such as *The Devil's Twin, The Apache Raider* and *Border*

Jack Perrin, Bullet and Leo greet Wally Wales in Presidio Productions' Overland Bound.

Blackbirds were filled with tense melodrama, excitement and suspense, providing a well-spent hour's entertainment for the western fan. But by this time, Maloney was fighting a losing battle; Pathé was fading into bankruptcy and Leo suffered a temporary eclipse in popularity after Joseph P. Kennedy shuttered its corral. In the summer of 1929, he directed *Overland Bound* for his Presidio Productions, the first of the independent all-talking westerns, and advance previews brought very kind words from the critics. But Leo never lived to enjoy his rebirth at the box-office; while in New York City to arrange for its distribution, 41-year-old Leo Maloney suffered a fatal stroke on November 1, 1929. His contribution to the western genre can best be summed up with the word integrity. In a field where anything went, as long as it earned money, Leo Maloney felt an obligation to produce pictures in the best way possible; formula pictures to be sure, but ones that his fans would always enjoy and his independent westerns showed this feeling where it counted most—on the screen.

Ken Maynard

Many western stars rode across the silent screen in the twenties, but few stood as tall in the saddle as one young Texan who ran away from home when he was 14 and who just might have been the greatest trick rider of all time, Ken Maynard. Ken came to the movies in December 1922, a 27-year old veteran of the circus-wild west show circuits whose riding and roping abilities were just short of astonishing and caught the eye of Lynn Reynolds, one of Tom Mix's directors at Fox. Ken was in Los Angeles at the time, performing as a featured rider with the Ringling Brothers-Barnum and Bailey Circus.

His picture career might never have come to pass had Ken waited for Fox to put him to work. Charles "Buck" Jones, who had been brought in to help keep Tom Mix under tight rein two years before, was now clearly destined for stardom. Taking a hard line over his contract and options, Jones had joined Tom in giving William Fox something to worry about. Maynard was to be the threat which Fox would use if necessary to keep his two stars in line, but everything was finally settled amicably and Ken sat out his option, appearing but briefly in one film before moving on to pick up bit roles in other pictures.

Late in 1923, Ken signed with Clifford S. Elfelt Productions for a series of eight independent westerns. J. Charles Davis II, a one-time executive at Arrow and now Elfelt's general sales manager, was sufficiently alert to Maynard's box-office potential to buy the series for release by his own Davis Distributing Division. Beginning with *$50,000 Reward*, the series was a light-hearted attempt at comic melodrama and came off rather well. Probably the best remembered today is *The Grey Vulture*, in which Ken portrayed a young ranch hand so interested in the history of the Middle Ages that he fancied himself a knight on horseback out to do battle with the forces of evil for the hand of the fair maiden, who really wanted nothing to do with him. Other films in this group were as

Ken Maynard.

The Grey Vulture.

Ken behind a mask in **The Unknown Cavalier.**

appropriately named (*The Demon Rider, Haunted Range*) and several served as a showcase for the Hollywood Beauty Sextette, a group of shapely and aspiring starlets who lent their attractive charms in support of our handsome lantern-jawed hero. Although a bit off the beaten track, this series gave the young Texan enough exposure to bring him to the attention of First National and the beginning of a lengthy and profitable association with producer Harry Joe Brown. Under Brown's guidance, Ken Maynard's popularity with audiences quickly rivaled that of Mix, Jones and Hoot Gibson. The eight for Elfelt would later be recut into a rather incoherent 10-episode serial retitled *The Range Fighter* and reissued once Ken was a box-office attraction.

The Ken Maynard First National westerns were rather elaborately mounted productions, and like the M-G-M Tim McCoy westerns they showed what could be done with $75,000 when it was properly spent. The stories were first rate and written to feature Ken's outstanding riding as an integral part of the plot. Good supporting casts were generally provided and it mattered little whether or not Maynard could really act. After several years of westerns that

Somewhere in Sonora.

had moved at a snail's pace, along came a star whose films breathed action from the opening title and they catapulted Ken to the top ranks of western stardom.

Unlike several other western heroes created at about the same time (Buffalo Bill Jr., Wally Wales, Buddy Roosevelt), Ken had the distinct advantage of release by First National and play dates in the bigger and better theatres as a result. As in the case of Colonel Tim McCoy, this factor in his success was not to be taken lightly; the same films released by Weiss Brothers Artclass or even Pathé would have reached a different audience and could not have placed Ken as firmly in the public eye as did his association with First National.

While many of the other directors grinding out westerns relied on long and medium shots to establish and play out the action, Al Rogell brought Sol Polito's camera in tight on Ken in several running inserts and watching a western like *The Red Raiders* today is as refreshing as it must have been in 1927. A Cavalry picture teeming with the action of an Indian war on the plains, framed by attractive backgrounds and a large complement of Crow

Ken Maynard and Harry Joe Brown, who guided the star's rise to fame and fortune in the twenties.

Indians playing Apaches, *The Red Raiders* was a perfect vehicle for Maynard. Although he didn't direct it, J. P. McGowan found time to play Ken's superior officer and romantic rival for Ann Drew, who turned out to be about as colorless a western heroine as the screen ever featured. Paul Hurst dropped his usual villainy long enough to play the hard-bitten topkick in the same vein later essayed so well by J. C. Flippen in so many talkie cavalry sagas.

But the most spectacular features of Ken's westerns were the

Virginia Lee Corbin, Strongheart and Ken in North Star, *1926.*

Ken in a scene from The Range Fighter, *a serial constructed from his early western series for Charles Elfelt.*

The Range Fighter, *Episode #2—Trapped.*

A production still from The Red Raiders *(1926) with Ken and Chief Yowlache. This scene does not appear in existing prints of the film.*

constant emphasis on action, strong story lines and Ken's own trick riding. With the camera in close enough to reveal that Maynard was not being doubled in his early films, fans took an instant liking to this good-looking hero, whose bashful reticence with the heroine failed to slow the pacing of his pictures and Ken Maynard continued his celluloid adventures at First National until 1929, when sound forced every production firm to reevaluate its position. Ken and First National did not see eye-to-eye on several things and the star moved over to Universal where he was given his own production unit. Harry J. Brown and scripter Marion Jackson followed.

Ken's Universal westerns were made as silents with some dialogue sections added using sound-on-discs. In order to market these in the theatres wired for sound, the rest of each picture carried a musical background. Released in both versions, Universal made the grand mistake of selling them to exhibitors as "100 percent talking pictures" and theatre owners screamed in dismay when they screened the Maynard series, complaining that the sound was of poor quality and the background music so loud that it inter-

The Upland Rider.

The Royal Rider.

fered in some places with the dialogue, to say nothing of the outright deception involved in advertising and selling the series as talkies. The silent versions of at least three from this group are in existence today, and although not up to the quality of his First National series, *Senior Americano,* *Lucky Larkin* and *The Fighting Legion* are outstanding westerns, when you consider the general quality of the westerns made during this transitional period; most of the competition was pretty bad.

Ken went on to make several series of independent westerns before turning up at Mascot in 1934–35, where his *Mystery Mountain* and *In Old Santa Fe* brought Gene Autry and Smiley Burnette to the western screen, beginning the cycle of musical westerns. But historically, Maynard holds the distinction of being the movies' first singing cowpoke; he introduced songs in his 1929–30 sound-on-disc Universal series. But Ken's singing, like his trick riding, was done as an integral part of the story, unlike the "I'll sing if you drop a hat" westerns which made Republic and Herbert J. Yates wealthy.

Unfortunately, Ken's sound westerns suffered from his own heavy hand as producer-director-writer-star and his popularity during the thirties dropped well below that of a top star. Many of his friends felt that his downfall began when Harry J. Brown and Marion Jackson finally left the unit, and it appears that there might be a strong element of truth in this judgment. But for the failure to let more experienced and knowledgable hands guide him, Maynard could easily have reigned as *the* western star of the era. By the time Ken hung up his screen spurs in 1944, he had earned an estimated $3 million and endeared himself to millions of youngsters around the world. What more could any performer ask? At the time of this writing, Ken Maynard lives quietly in a mobile home located in the San Fernando Valley, surrounded by memories of the two decades he spent as one of the most popular of the Winners of the West.

★★★

Tim McCoy

Born into a modestly prosperous Irish family in Saginaw, Michigan, as the last decade of the 19th century opened (and the frontier began to disappear), Timothy John Fitzgerald McCoy was to become the most authentic of the celluloid cowboys in the twenties. Through his father's eloquent accounts of the Civil War and Gettysburg, and by acquaintance with a local merchant who imported wranglers to handle his horses, young Tim McCoy developed an early and lasting interest in both history and the West.

Leaving Chicago and St. Ignatius College in 1912, Tim shut the door on formal education to take Horace Greeley's advice. Heading West, he stopped only when his bankroll had dwindled to a single $5.00 bill. This placed him in Lander, Wyoming, where he found work on a nearby ranch and applied for a homestead near the Wind River. Once the home of the proud Shoshone and Arapahoe, the Wind River Country was still wilderness, and to locate lost cattle Tim found it necessary to learn the Indian's sign language.

When America entered the First World War, an enthusiastic McCoy wired Theodore Roosevelt that he would raise a troop of cavalry for the contingent that Teddy had offered President Wilson. Roosevelt was delighted with Tim's offer but the War Department had reservations about turning an aging Boy Scout loose on the battlefields of France and tactfully refused the old Rough Rider permission to carry out his plans. But Tim was commissioned a captain and assigned to the staff of General Hugh Scott. Their common interest in the Indian gave the General and his captain the basis for a firm friendship and after the war ended, McCoy, now a colonel, returned to the Wind River country as Indian agent for the Bureau of Indian Affairs. By this time, Tim had thoroughly investigated Custer's disaster at The Little Big Horn and was regarded as one of the outstanding authorities on the American Indian.

Colonel Tim McCoy.

Tim McCoy's entrance into the make-believe world of motion pictures came in a manner similar to that of Tom Mix. In need of 500 long-haired Indians to add authenticity to his production of Emerson Hough's *The Covered Wagon* in 1922, Jesse Lasky asked the Indian Bureau for help. As agent at the Wind River Reservation, the one nearest to the picture's location filming, Tim was requested to furnish the Indians and serve as interpreter during their stay. As these extras were wards of the federal government, McCoy's

Tim dances with Pauline Starke in War Paint, *his first starring role for M-G-M.*

Tim McCoy's M-G-M westerns were well-staged pageants of American history. Here he gallantly escorts a youthful Joan Crawford in Winners of the Wilderness.

The famous McCoy profile with Pauline Starke. From War Paint, *1926.*

Reginald Barker directed several of the McCoy westerns. Tim chooses his weapon on the set of The Frontiersman, *as Louise Lorraine looks on.*

sole responsibility required him to make certain that they were not mistreated, but he soon found himself cast in another role.

Watching an actor on the set hitch up a team of oxen and realizing that the poor fellow obviously didn't have the slightest idea of what he was trying to do, Tim quickly taught him the proper method. Director James Cruze stood nearby watching and, impressed with McCoy's knowledgeable self-assurance, asked him to serve as the picture's technical advisor. When it premiered in 1923 at Grauman's Chinese Theatre in Hollywood, Colonel Tim McCoy supervised a display of Indian and historical material and presented a prologue on-stage. Pleased with its reception, Lasky asked him to repeat the exhibit for the London premiere. Tim accepted, resigned both his commission and job and stayed on in London with the show for over a year.

When McCoy returned to the United States after finishing his public relations stint for Paramount, he worked on their lot as technical advisor during the production of *The Thundering Herd*

The Frontiersman *told the story of the Seminole Indian Wars. Tim informs Louise Lorraine that he must leave to join General Andrew Jackson.*

(in which he also played a supporting role) and *The Vanishing American*. But someone at M-G-M recognized a potential in this tall, handsome real-life hero and signed him to a contract. W. S. Van Dyke, a director noted for his low-budget and fast-action films with Buck Jones, was brought in, and in the fall of 1926 Tim McCoy appeared on the screen with Pauline Starke in his first of 17 M-G-M westerns, *War Paint*, a story Van Dyke had put together off-the-cuff.

Why did Tim McCoy leave an altogether satisfactory life for the uncertainty of an acting career? The novelty was partly responsible (Tim was a great ham), as was the money; but mainly it was his deep and abiding interest in western history and lore, which had deviated considerably on-screen from the realism of Bill Hart. Hart had reached the end of a long trail with no successor stylistically and Tim thought he saw a chance to publicize the plight of the Red Man via the screen.

Anxious to shake the reputation he had acquired, Woody Van Dyke tried quality as a stepping stone to bigger things, but when it failed to bring the recognition he sought from the front office, Van Dyke fell back on that which he knew best—fast action and reduced costs—as a means to his end. It would work; his efforts with McCoy convinced Irving Thalberg that Van Dyke was the man to do *Trader Horn* in the early days of sound. But even so, the Tim McCoy westerns for M-G-M were without a doubt the best of their kind in the late twenties, exceeding in production values even the excellent Ken Maynard series for First National. *California* related the story of the 1845 war between the United States and Mexico, culminating with the admission to statehood; *The Frontiersman* concerned Andrew Jackson and the Creek Indian uprising; *Winners of the Wilderness* told the story of colonial days and a French attempt to conquer the Ohio Valley.

Directed mainly by Van Dyke and Reginald Barker, McCoy's features were somewhat slow in pacing, with the action sequences widely separated by plot development. M-G-M reputedly budgeted them at $80,000 (of which Tim was paid $4,000), a low figure for that company's product but expensive when compared with many of the other westerns of the period, especially the independents. With an eye toward authenticity, this expenditure allowed lavish costuming by competitors' standards (although McCoy much preferred simple dress, especially buckskins) and the use of competent, well-known actresses as feminine leads—Claire Windsor, Louise Lorraine, Racquel Torres and Dorothy Sebastian, as well as a youthful Joan Crawford and starlet Jean Arthur.

Although a bit stiff-necked in his acting, Tim developed into a pleasing personality on-screen, and ham that he was mastered

Captured by the Indians after joining Jackson in **The Frontiersman,** *Tim received the standard cinematic ceremony of welcome.*

the grand entrance—saloon doors thrown wide open to reveal the somber personage, eyes quickly scanning and rescanning the interior before venturing beyond the door. The kids loved him for it. The saloon entrance and his gunfight scenes were Tim McCoy at his best. The originator of the gun-fanning style of shooting, he also had a knack of throwing his gun when he shot, as if he were actually pumping lead, and screen cowboys of the thirties quickly adopted it as their own.

Van Dyke soon acquired an assistant in the person of David Selznick and the two came up with a scheme to make themselves look good in the eyes of the front office. While it was not unusual to shoot westerns "back-to-back" (one directly following the other using the same sets and locations), Van Dyke and Selznick decided to shoot McCoy's "side-by-side." Using two different camera setups, they shuttled their star back and forth between sets and were able to put two films in the can at the same time for a total cost of about $90,000, or a saving of $70,000 per pair. Surprisingly, the quality of Tim's films did not suffer greatly as a result of this production innovation, but the star did get very tired of making

Tim's westerns were well advertised with exciting posters.

two at a time and when sound forced M-G-M to reconsider its position regarding westerns, McCoy was pleased. He joined Universal, appearing with serial queen Aileen Ray in the first of two chapter plays he would make, *The Indians Are Coming*.

Made in two versions, this 12-episode serial had the distinction of being the first of the talking serials, as well as the last of the silents. While not a particularly good chapter play from its story angle, it was a technical achievement and the first of its kind to play the Roxy, grossing many times its modest $160,000 investment and giving the serial genre a new lease on life.

Tim went on to greater glory in the thirties and became one

The famous McCoy stare, complete with six-shooter.

of the few western stars to successfully intermix his work for both major studios and independents, with no apparent ill effects on his career. In 1935, he took to the road with the Sells-Floto division of Ringling Brothers-Barnum and Bailey Combined Shows, replacing Tom Mix; and in 1938 he opened his own Wild West Show. It lasted but 28 days, went bankrupt in Washington and cost Tim $100,000. It was back to the screen for McCoy but when television opened up new vistas, Tim hosted his own show for a time and dealt with western history in his own inimitable fashion. Semi-retired at this writing, Tim McCoy's last screen appearance came in Alex Gordon's 1965 *Requiem for a Gunfighter*, and when his steel-eyed, grim-jawed visage appeared on the wide screen, there was no doubt about it—the Colonel was still one of the greatest of them all.

Tom Mix

(AMERICA'S CHAMPION COWBOY)

While it was Bill Hart who became *the* legendary western hero, it is quite unlikely that any sagebrush hero ever rode across the screen enjoying a popularity equal to that of Tom Mix. Hart, whose westerns reeked with the realism of the old West, had captivated a generation of fans for a decade and won the praise of usually caustic critics, but failed to match either the box-office draw or longevity of reign that characterized the seemingly-ageless Mix. Jack Natteford, who worked with both, once estimated that while Hart earned approximately $4 million in his career, Mix brought home over $7.5 million in wages. Tom's credentials were impressive enough; he came to the screen after cramming several lifetimes into his 30 years. Veteran of the Spanish-American War, Philippine Insurrection and Boxer Rebellion, Deputy U.S. Marshal, Texas Ranger, soldier-of-fortune—he had been all these and more, according to the legend.

Tom's association with the movies began in 1910 when he offered the use of his ranch to the Selig Polyscope Company for filming westerns. Selig accepted and the footage captured by his camera crew was released as *Ranch Life in the Great Southwest*. During the filming, Mix had acted as general advisor for the documentary and left at its conclusion to join Madero's revolution in Mexico. Returning to the United States after several harrowing experiences below the border, Tom discovered much to his surprise that Selig had been trying to locate him. Rejoining the producer's staff as an animal handler and double, Mix eventually stepped before the camera himself, and by 1911 had become a permanent member of Selig's California studio, where he wrote, directed and starred in several hundred single and multiple-reel westerns between 1911–17.

While the majority of his shorter films were uneven in quality, a reflection both of Selig's concern for money and Tom's lack of

America's Champion Cowboy.

experience in the dramatic arts (a sizeable portion can even be considered as western comedies), Tom's real impact came in his multiple-reel pictures, such as *In the Days of the Thundering Herd* (1913) and *Chip of the Flying U* (1914). Containing action and adventure on a scale surpassed only in the Kay-Bee westerns made by Thomas H. Ince, these five-reel features were directed by Colin Campbell, perhaps the most talented of Selig's directors, and pro-

Tom, Victoria Forde, Pat Chrisman and Sid Jordan in Local Color, *one of the Mix shorts for Selig.*

vided excellent showcases for Tom's colorful handling of horse, lariat and gun. But however good or bad it was, this vast outpouring of Tom Mix films for Selig served its purpose, establishing him as a popular favorite with fans and providing a fine training ground for the immediate stardom he would enjoy at Fox in 1917.

Tom's first few films for Fox were two-reelers, written and directed by himself, but wisely leaving the writing and direction

Sid Jordan and Tom Mix in one of his final two-reelers, **The Roman Cowboy,** *made shortly after joining Fox.*

of his feature-length pictures to those more qualified, Mix set out to create a West somewhat different from the one portrayed by Broncho Billy and William S. Hart. There was a *joie de vivre* in Tom Mix that came across on the screen and not a single rival was ever really able to re-create it in their own image. Within two years, Mix had overtaken the declining Hart at the box-office and began his reign as "America's Champion Cowboy," making Fox wealthy in the process and replacing Theda Bara as the source of financial support for such expensive failures as the features made with the former Pathé serial queen, Pearl White. Without a doubt, Tom's contract with Fox was the most profitable piece of paper ever signed by either man.

While some of the westerns Mix made for Fox were light-hearted affairs, most were fast-moving, exciting slices of entertainment (*The Rainbow Trail, The Great K & A Train Robbery* and *The Lone Star Ranger*), which featured logically motivated action played against a backdrop of superior location footage, much of which was shot in National Parks. Unlike Anderson and Hart before him, Tom avoided the "good-badman" and western dude portrayals, preferring

Tom and Tony in Do and Dare.

The excellent horsemanship of Tom Mix provided many thrilling moments for his youthful admirers in Do and Dare.

Setting himself apart from the tradition established by William S. Hart, Tom favored fancy western dress, as in this scene from Prairie Trails *with Charles K. French and Kathleen O'Connor.*

instead to keep close to his concept of the hero as one who became inadvertantly involved while lending others a helping hand. His primary audience interest seems to have been his young fans, for Tom's later screen character eschewed violence and killing except as a last resort, and in his days at Fox, Mix refrained from offending us by swearing, drinking and carousing, or succumbing to the tender embraces of the leading lady, as he had in the multitude of Selig films.

Tom's westerns were superior examples of formula pictures developed to a pitch of perfection by some of the most skillful directors in the business. In his decade with Fox, Mix worked with a dozen of the best, including Lambert Hillyer, John Ford and George Marshall. Scripting was on par with the direction and Dan Clark's superbly crisp and beautiful photography put feature after feature in the can, each one guaranteed to bring the audience back for more. By 1925, Tom Mix was earning (and spending) $17,000 weekly.

Kathleen O'Connor has Tom exactly where she wants him in **Prairie Trails.**

Tom did much of his own stunt work, something he was exceptionally proud of in a day and age when lesser stars were contented to step before the camera for close-ups, leaving the dangerous work to stunt doubles. Tom Mix was too much of a showman to sit by idle while others did his work and too proud to rest on his laurels; the scars which covered his body were mute testimony to this fact. Mix left Fox in 1928 to join Film Booking Office (FBO), turning out a half-dozen pictures in a vein similar to his Fox westerns before sound arrived.

Although the change-over from silents to talkies hurt the western in the early thirties, it didn't upset Tom, who began his third decade in show business touring the country with the Sells-Floto division of Ringling Brothers-Barnum and Bailey Combined Shows. His salary of $10,000 weekly meant a cutback in his living style, but Mix still lived lavishly, very much so for the period. Tom made but one series of features in the thirties; Universal put him under contract in 1932–33 for a group of nine features. All

One word from Tom and Robert Walker's tie will need readjusting in The Texan.

The Yankee Senor.

The Great K & A Train Robbery *blended humor with the usual Mix thrills.*

Even though Tom was in his fifties, his talkies for Universal lacked none of the action associated with his silent westerns, as demonstrated in The Texas Bad Man, *1932.*

The Mix westerns were filmed on location and included some of the most spectacular scenery put on film in the silent westerns. This sequence from The Great K & A Train Robbery *was filmed on location in the Royal Gorge of the Colorado River.*

were enjoyable and well done and while legend has it that the star's dialogue came across slurred and unconvincing, nothing could be further from the truth; the deep baritone voice of Tom Mix delivered its lines in a professional and believable manner in such films as *Destry Rides Again, Flaming Guns* and *Riders of Death Valley.*

Tom chose to end his screen career in 1935 with a rather undistinguished Mascot serial, *The Miracle Rider* but movies were no longer Tom's sole interest—he was well past the age when a man looked forward to the hard work involved in filming an action-packed five reels and while he had been absent from the screen much of the time during the early thirties, licensees had kept his name before the public with toys and clothing merchandised as "Approved by Tom Mix." The first western star to exploit his name in this manner, Tom was also the first to conquer the medium of radio.

The Tom Mix radio series first aired in 1933. Early chapters used his real life as well as the one he had led on-screen for its basis and the Ralston people (his sponsors) clapped their hands in glee—*Tom Mix* began a 17-year run, outliving its namesake by a decade. Star that he was, Tom refused to do the show himself—radio salaries were too small and he had the Tom Mix Wild West Circus to think about; its organizers had paid well for the use of his name.

I saw Tom Mix but once in person; during the fall of 1939 he appeared on stage at the Playhouse in Enosburg, Vermont, and to those of us who numbered among his youthful admirers, the world was never the same after that night. No matter that he was almost 60 years old and would die a year later in a tragic automobile accident in Arizona—the tall masculine figure dressed in solid white and wearing his huge sombrero and shiny black boots would remain that way forever in our memories—"America's Champion Cowboy."

★★

Pete Morrison

In the early days of the picture business, exhibitors were unable to get sufficient films to keep their customers happy; no matter how many were produced, the market could absorb more and this unusual state of affairs created countless job opportunities for actors. While the legitimate stage and even vaudeville were fairly rigid structures by the turn of the century—few personalities began at the top—the emerging motion picture industry allowed anyone to start as a leading man. Starring roles were usually given to those who were at least blessed with the minimum of a pleasing personality and appearance on-screen; talent and luck operated to separate the various levels of stardom.

George D. (Pete) Morrison came to the movies in 1908 at the age of 15, beginning a career that would take him from extra to leading man and back again, spanning several decades along the way. Born and raised in Denver, Pete found work as an extra with a Selig unit that had been sent to Colorado to film westerns, and the tall, husky kid who looked like a leading man quickly became one. Over the next 10 years, he worked for Pathé, Essanay, American, Triangle and Universal (the home of the assembly-line western), alternating between leads and supporting roles.

The creation of Carl Laemmle, immigrant and one-time clothing merchant, Universal was not in the movie business for glory. Contented to let William Fox, Adolph Zukor and Marcus Loew battle each other for prestige, Laemmle was interested only in money, and to get it he put together an organization unrivaled in its ability to grind out films, most of which would have to be considered as "B" pictures. As George Marshall remarked, "There was no question about good or bad pictures at the time. Universal's several brands released a specified number each year; exhibitors bought them all and cried for more. You could sell anything you could film in those days and the demand for product made leading men of character actors like Pete. There was little question about talent at

Pete Morrison

Universal (and many other lots), it was simply a question of filling the main parts with someone who photographed well and then directing the daylights out of them. Pete was tall, good-looking and took direction well—what more could you ask?"

Universal produced several series of western short subjects in the World War I period and immediately thereafter. Two-reelers were in great demand in the second- and third-run houses and served as a jumping-off point for the careers of several western actors, with Art Acord, Harry Carey and Hoot Gibson among the most famous alumni. Others like Ed Cobb and Pete found their way into features for awhile and a few like Bob Burns never made it at all.

Pete left Universal in early 1921 to appear in a series of two-reel "specials" to be made by Daniel F. Tattenham (a former exhibitor turned producer) and released monthly by Independent

Pete points the finger in **The Escape.**

Morrison's flair for light comedy was put to good use in "Bucking The Truth", 1926.

Making Good.

The return of Texas Pat.

Entering pictures in their early days, Pete appeared in hundreds of short westerns and features, but he never made it into the ranks of the top stars. This scene is from Bucking the Truth.

Films Association. The first of the series, *The Long Trail*, appeared in April, and the following month Pete signed with director Cliff Smith. Smith had established his own company to make eight features for state-right release by Associated Photoplays (some were eventually marketed by the American Releasing Corporation) and Naida Carl and Al Kaufman came aboard as leading lady and heavy.

The Smith westerns were quite predictable for their time. Although conventional in plot, the usual elements of characterization, dramatic climax, sentiment and side issues were thrown to the winds. All that remained was virtue, which triumphed over villainy with a surprising economy of conflict and the script developed a simple plot line in a linear fashion. *Crossing Trails* was a good example and stands today as one of the few Morrison features available for viewing. The heroine escaped the villain by hiding on Pete's ranch and he took it from there in a series of incidents designed to foil the heavy. Chases played a large role (one after each attempt on the girl's life) and the five-reeler proved to be a good substitute for a short serial. The single element that seemed

Morrison, as he appeared in the late twenties.

to set the Cliff Smith-Pete Morrison collaboration above its competition was the way in which Pete handled his role. Discovering his star to be adept at light comedy, Smith developed Morrison's role with a touch of burlesque instead of playing it completely straight.

Finishing his series with Smith, Pete replaced William Fairbanks at Western Feature Productions (Fairbanks had jumped his contract), where he costarred with Dorothy Woods during 1922–23 in a group of lighthearted films, none of which taxed the imagination and/or ingenuity of their script writers. But these Sanford releases served to bring Morrison back to Universal in mid-1923 to make *Ghost City*, a 15-episode serial. A short series for Steiner release in 1924 was followed by several westerns for Harry Webb's Lariat Productions in 1925. Pete's importance as a western star ended with an interesting group of Blue Streak westerns for Universal in 1925–26 (*Blue Blazes, Chasing Trouble, The Desperate Game*). Written by Frank Beresford, these serio-comic westerns were directed by Milburn Morante, one of the least-talented of the silent comedians, and came off surprisingly well. More of a straight man than a comic, Morante had turned to production in the early twenties and proved to be much better at directing the comic talents of others.

Pete's Universal series contained a keen blend of light comedy and serious melodrama, but the curtain was preparing to close on his starring career. By the time sound arrived, Morrison had slipped rather easily back into secondary roles, supporting Yakima Canutt in his Bell Pictures during 1929. His boyish appearance had not stood advancing age as well as some of his contemporaries, and as Pete put on weight he turned into the ideal heavy for the independent oaters of the thirties. Extra to leading man and back again—the world comes full circle.

Jack Perrin

Success as a celluloid cowboy came a good deal easier in the twenties than it did a decade later; at least that was the opinion of one make-believe westerner who enjoyed a modest starring career catering to the thrill-hungry audiences of the neighborhood theatres during the heyday of the silent western. Although he played a great variety of roles during his lengthy screen career, Jack Perrin was primarily identified with his western roles.

Young Jack's fascination with movies began after graduation from high school with a job sweeping floors at Mack Sennett's "Fun Factory," but he was soon moved in front of the camera wearing the uniform of a Keystone Kop. Comedy did not seem to be his forte, especially the knockabout slapstick of Keystone, and so Perrin looked elsewhere for work. He finally landed a small role in Triangle's *Toton the Apache* in 1917, but shortly after completing this he and a group of friends decided that a hitch in the submarine service would be a real lark and Jack spent World War I working for Uncle Sam.

Release from military service in 1919 brought him back to Hollywood, a wiser and more determined young man. Universal was just beginning to expand its short-subject production and Jack landed a contract, appearing as a juvenile heavy in a few of Eddie Polo's "Cyclone Smith" two-reelers. While at Universal, he learned that versatility was good insurance for survival in the celluloid jungle and turned up playing every type of role from light comedy to deep drama.

When Jack was given the leading role in *The Lion Man*, an 18-episode serial, it looked as if his big opportunity had finally arrived; but this chapter play (filmed in Bronson Canyon where Jack had several close calls working without a stuntman to double him) featured J. Barney Sherry as a mysterious figure whose features were hidden behind a replica of a lion's head and the mask (and Mack Wright's stunting) stole the audience interest and

Jack Perrin.

the picture. As a result of this experience, Perrin soon discovered that his handsome profile was somewhat of a liability; unless playing a society role, Jack invariably looked like a miscast fashion plate.

After working for Metro, Arrow, FBO, Associated Exhibitors and First National in a variety of roles, his starring career in westerns began in the early twenties with a series for independent producer Harry Webb. Watching his films today, there seems to be an air of unreality surrounding Jack Perrin on the screen—he was

A gentleman cowboy, Perrin was always immaculate on-screen. With Jack Rockwell and Ethlyne Clair from Guardians of the Wild.

just too handsome, too neat and too virtuous to be a real western he-man, as one envisions them today. Other sagebrush heroes were also neat in appearance on-screen, but Perrin was one of those oft-envied fellows who looked well-dressed in rags, and as a result appeared just a trifle too fastidious to be real. While violent enough to suit anyone in the audiences, Jack's fist fights saw him emerge the victor time after time, with unmussed clothes and a white Stetson still covering a head of neatly combed hair.

Although the Jack Perrin westerns were always entertaining, they were seldom convincing. He was too predictable a hero, representing a set of values in the process of change. He (or his script writers) also seemed to have fascination for two types of roles—the Texas Ranger in disguise and the Marine who turned up out West, complete with full-dress uniform. Perrin's several series for Harry Webb were released by Rayart and Jack also made a number of westerns for Awyon during the same period. Fans who wanted to see this busy star badly enough were never very far from a Jack Perrin western during 1923–26.

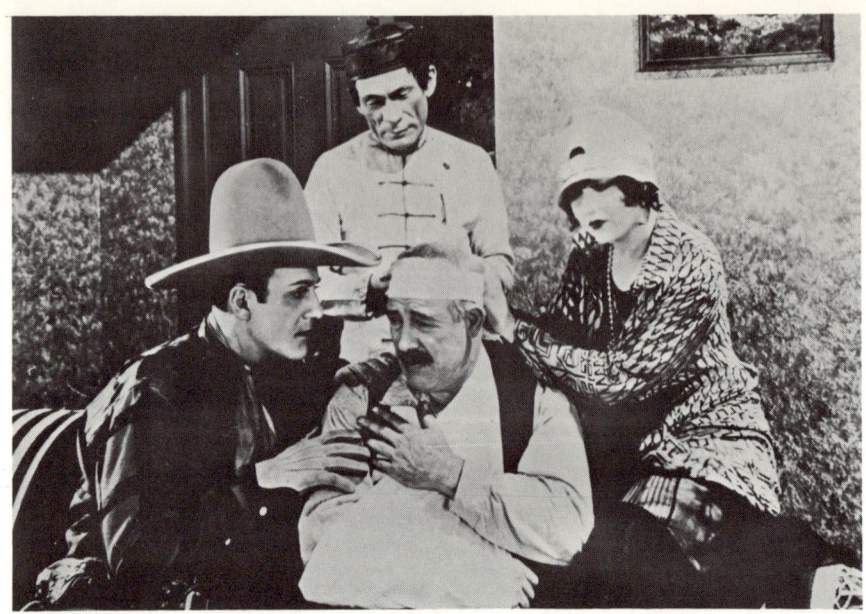

Jack and Ethlyne Clair in Guardians of The Wild.

Jack and Louise Lorraine.

Tom London has it in for Jack in Universal's **Harvest of Hate.**

Jack's best work during these years came in his final (1926) Rayart series (*Knockout Kid, The Thunderbolt Strikes, Man From Oklahoma, West of Rainbow's End*), which featured little Billy Lamar and Molly Malone in support. A miniature whirlwind on horseback, Billy would shortly find his own brief stardom as "Buzz" Barton in an FBO series. Perrin left the West briefly in 1927, filming *Fire and Steel,* a story of the steel industry, for Elbee Pictures, but by May, Jack was on the range once more, this time back at Universal where he had started almost a decade before. He starred

Jack in Ridin' Law, *one of his early talkie appearances.*

in the *Northwest Mounted Police* series, a group of above-average two-reel short subjects directed by Josef Levigard. Fast-moving dramas from the pens of Arthur Henry Gooden and Basil Dickey, *Yukon Gold, Madden of The Mounted* and *King of Hearts* were among the best of a series which put Jack Perrin back in features during 1929.

Our stalwart hero made four good features for Universal that year (*Harvest of Hate, Hoofbeats of Vengeance, Plunging Hoofs, Wild Blood*) and then costarred with Leo Maloney in his independent talkie western, *Overland Bound*. This was Jack's first experience with sound and proved to be a technical nightmare. Using sound-on-discs, the cast was required to go through their scenes in five-minute blocks with no mistakes. The riding sequences were shot silent, with sound effects added later in the form of coconut shells simulating hoofbeats. Although quite primitive, *Overland Bound* did receive good reviews, but Leo Maloney had died in New York while arranging for its release and the film never was given adequate distribution.

Jack's last silent appearance came in *The Jade Box*, a non-western serial for Universal to which music and sound effects

The mid-thirties found Perrin reduced to supporting roles in the westerns of second-string sagebrush stars like Bob Allen. Here he faces Jack Rockwell in Reckless Ranger, *one of Allen's talkies.*

Cactus Trails.

were added as an afterthought. It was not a great box-office success and Universal dropped his contract option. But Jack was a good horseman and with a suitable voice for talkies, he set out to conquer the new medium. In a field already overcrowded with both old-timers and aspiring newcomers, Jack Perrin found work only in independent westerns. Gradually, he slipped back to supporting roles and then character parts, with television giving his career a brief boost just before he retired.

Jack's last years were spent in the declining health of old age, but he enjoyed recalling the good days when he rode tall in the saddle, willingly sharing his experiences with anyone who was interested right up until his death in 1968. Television has given us a new breed of western hero, whose character may well be closer to reality, but to those who remember the days when the forces of good were personified on the screen by the Jack Perrins, there's really no comparison.

Buddy Roosevelt

(THE RIDING FOOL)

Some western actors found the road to stardom a quick and easy one; for those without either talent or personality, it never really existed. But while the possession of one or both of these requirements was a necessity, it was not a sure-fire guarantee that producers or the public would recognize the qualifications immediately; for a few, perseverance was also a desired quality. Buddy Roosevelt persevered for almost a decade before he found the trail to the top.

The son of a judge in Rio Blanco County, Colorado, Buddy was born Kent Sanderson in 1898. Judge Sanderson made his home on a ranch near Meeker, where Kent learned to rope and ride at an early age. Wanting his son to study law, the judge sent him to Boston to study at Cambridge Tech, but Kent had other ideas. Once billed as Charlotte Spooner, his mother had been a modestly successful opera singer and young Sanderson was captivated by the prospects of a career in the entertainment world. Leaving his formal education behind, Kent turned to that which he knew best and joined the C. B. Irwin Wild West Show as a stunt rider.

It was only a short time before he arrived in Los Angeles and headed for the studios. But this was 1915 and Hollywood was filled with stunt men and daredevil cowboys willing to risk their necks for a day's work—the arrival of another meant nothing to the film capital and so Kent Sanderson became a night dishwasher in the Methodist Hospital in Los Angeles. His days were spent in Hollywood seeking some way to break into pictures, and finally the door to Inceville opened and Buddy became a stunt double at Triangle for Tom Ince's leading ladies. The high point of his stay at Triangle came with several stunts and crowd scenes in Bill Hart's *Hell's Hinges*.

Buddy Roosevelt.

World War I interrupted a career noted mainly for its bruises and after service in the Navy, Kent returned to Hollywood. But there was no brass band, no welcoming committee to greet him— no one had noticed his absence from the screen. To support himself, Kent chopped wood and did odd jobs until a production expansion at Universal City elevated him back to the status of stunt man. Few stunt doubles ever made it out of the saddle and into the ranks of leading men, but Kent stayed with it and when Norman Dawn offered him a sizable role in *The Lure of the Yukon,* at $350 a week, Kent quickly signed the contract. For the independent producer, an acquisition like Sanderson was a bargain at that price. Tall and handsome, Kent Sanderson was attractive to the ladies, needed no expensive double, and with more than sufficient ability in the saddle he was able to put on a good show with a minimum of retakes and wasted time. He had found an occasional leading role in two-reel Universal shorts (*Down in Texas*) but stardom continued to elude the persistent young man until his path crossed that of Lester F. Scott Jr. in 1924.

A budding movie producer, Scott and his father had chased an elusive will-o-the-wisp around half the world. Obsessed with the possibility of "striking it rich," the two had dabbled with every kind of "get-rich-quick" scheme, but to no avail. The motion picture was his latest. Possessing a keen mind for business but somewhat impractical at times, Scott had decided that a new western star was the answer and he decided to create one—the world would know him as "Buck Mix."

In Galveston, Texas, on an oil venture, he met a friend of the family in a touring stage company, Elizabeth Burbridge. Her

Joseph W. Girard, Buddy, Al Taylor and Peggy Montgomery in The Dangerous Dub, *1926.*

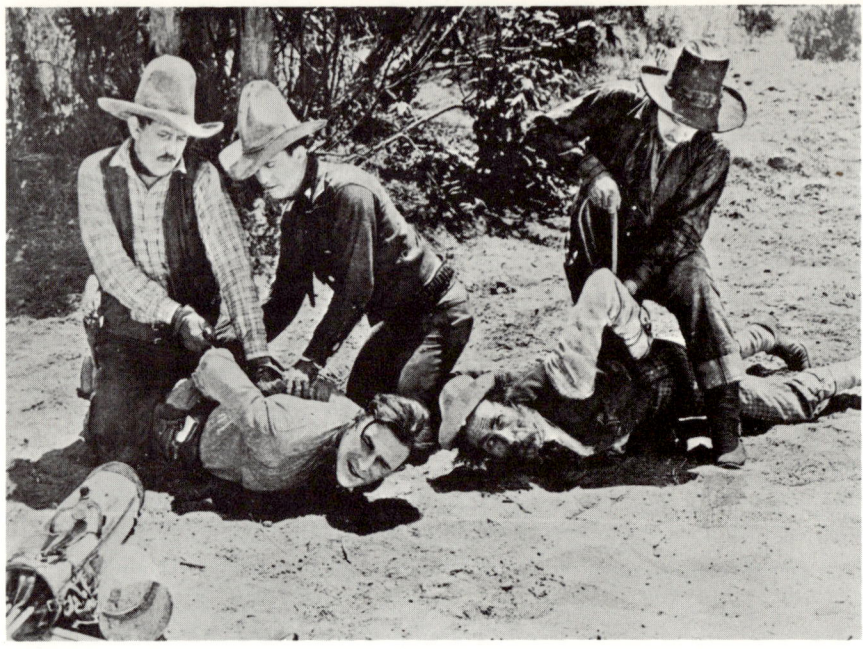

Buddy and Nelson McDowell are in trouble in **The Ramblin' Galoot,** *1926.*

experience included the movies and Scott talked her into creating a script for his proposed hero. Armed with the script and a $20,000 loan from his in-laws, Lester F. Scott Jr. was now president of Approved Pictures and Louis Weiss succumbed to his blandishments sufficiently to enter into a distribution contract. All Scott needed now was a warm body; he could see it on the screen—*Lester F. Scott Jr. Presents* . . . . Just watch the money roll in!

Scott's search came to an end with Kent Sanderson. Buck Mix was forgotten, but the beginning was almost the end for both Scott and Buddy. To direct this initial epic, Scott hired an eccentric named J. P. McCarthy, whose subsistence for several months had revolved around continuous promises to his landlady that his next job would make a star of the poor woman's daughter. True to his word, he saw that she was cast as the feminine lead and that the majority of Buddy's scenes wound up on the cutting room floor. Scott was forced to reshoot almost the entire picture to salvage it.

Rough Ridin', the first of what would be a long, unbroken series of starring roles for Kent Sanderson, alias Buddy Roosevelt, appeared in July 1924 and caustic reviewers, long accustomed to yawning with boredom at independent westerns, continued to yawn.

"Take mine," says Robert Homans to Buddy, as he hands him a gun in **The Bandit Buster,** *1926.*

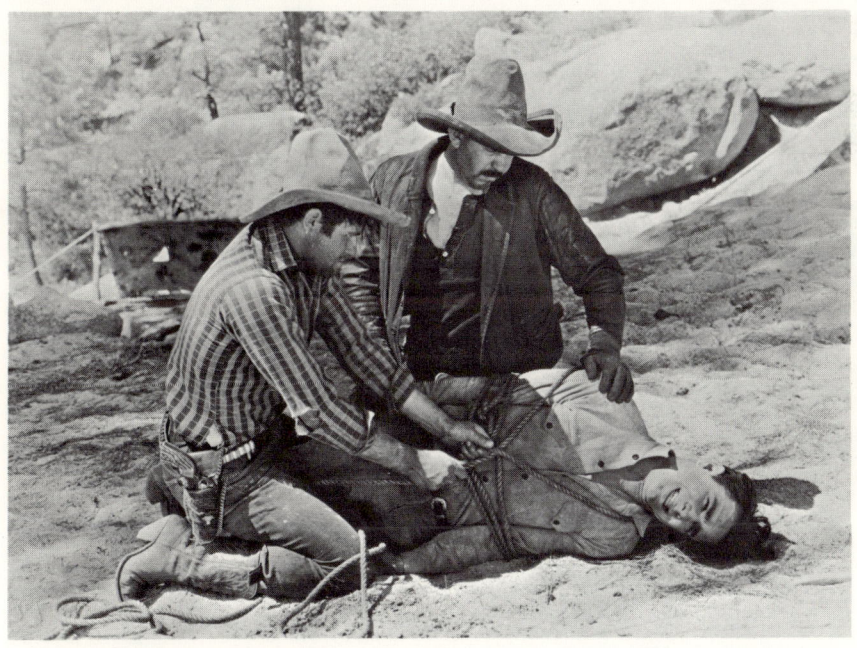

The gun didn't help Buddy; Tom Bay and Charles Whittaker got the drop on him anyway.

Robert Homans, Buddy, Molly Malone and Winifred Landis in The Bandit Buster.

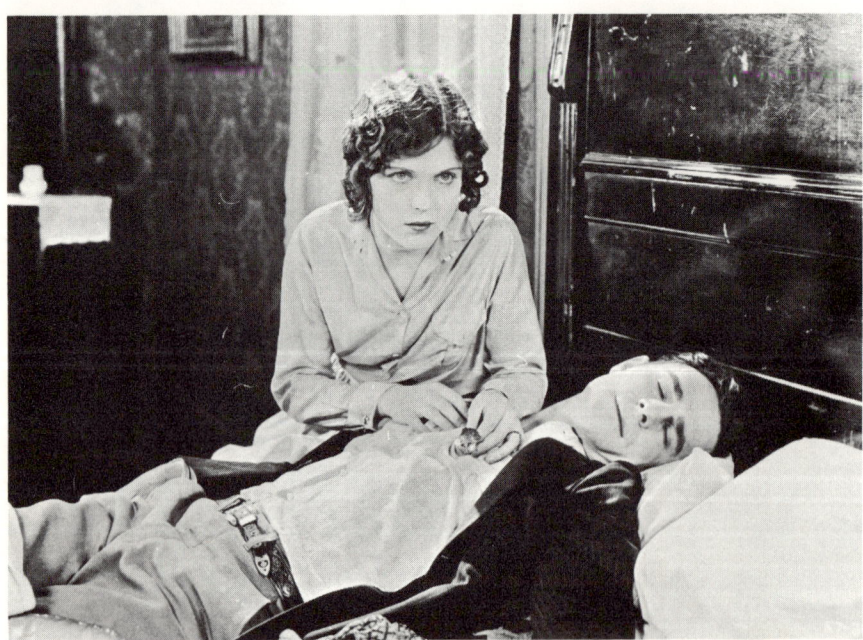

Alma Rayford discovers that the wounded Buddy is really a Ranger in The Phantom Buster, *1927.*

Buddy has Charles Whittaker (1) and henchmen under wraps in The Phantom Buster, *and no one ever took his prisoners away from Roosevelt.*

But fans thought differently and *Battling Buddy, Walloping Wallace* and *Rip-Roaring Roberts* followed in quick succession. Scott found himself drinking a toast to his good fortune—the Buddy Roosevelt series was making money. After the initial mishap, the direction of Buddy's films was entrusted to Richard Thorpe, who turned out to be Scott's resident wizard of the range. In addition to the monthly Roosevelt westerns, Thorpe also masterminded a similar release for the Buffalo Bill Jr. series, and later one with Wally Wales. He directed westerns night and day, awake and in his sleep. Betty Burbridge became chief story concocter, and while her schedule kept pace with that of Thorpe, she chuckles today when recalling that her duties at the time included reading stories, handling publicity, dreaming up new plot lines, adapting others and scripting three to four features each month, all for $65 a week.

The Buddy Roosevelt westerns were essentially action pictures, with fast and hard riding in every reel, interrupted by an occasional fist fight and brought to a close by a quick trigger finger. Although far from art, they were entertaining and Roosevelt's image on-screen rapidly developed into that of a respectable, God-fearing westerner who rolled with the punches only to come up fighting and win. Un-

Frank Ellis (1) restrains Buddy in Easy Going.

fortunately, his acting was not far above that of the majority of actors in independent westerns of the time; Buddy's personality was not transmitted well by the camera and his performance gave viewers the suspicion that he was not really at home in front of the camera. This fact is confirmed by Betty Burbridge, who recalls watching the daily rushes, "Buddy never loosened up until he heard the director yell 'cut.' At that moment, he relaxed completely and as the cameraman usually shot a few feet beyond the end of a scene, I was always amused by Buddy's lapse back to naturalness, a trait which would have improved his acting a great deal, had he retained it while the scene was being filmed."

In 1925, Approved Pictures renewed its Artclass contract and became Action Pictures. Buddy continued on Scott's payroll and watched his pictures move from the ignominy of Weiss Brothers' distribution to the prestige of Associated Exhibitors in 1926 and then to Pathé the following year. With Action Pictures growing, director Dick Thorpe was assigned to strengthen its other series, with Oscar Apfel and Tenny Wright taking over direction of the Roosevelt unit. But Thorpe didn't wander too far; under the pseudonym of Frank L. Inghram, he replaced Betty Burbridge as scenarist

When Pathé cancelled its contract for Buddy's Action Pictures, he moved to Trem Carr's unit at Rayart. One of the Rayart series, **The Trail Riders** *lacked the action of his earlier pictures.*

on the Roosevelt unit. Unfortunately for Buddy, Pathé was in the process of liquidating itself under the surgical prescription of Joseph P. Kennedy, and when Scott's contract for the Roosevelt series was not renewed in 1928, he fired the star, who immediately moved over to Trem Carr's studio to make a series for Rayart.

The Painted Trail, Trailing Back, Lightnin' Shot, Mystery Valley and others appeared in quick succession under the Rayart sunburst logo, but added nothing to the Buddy Roosevelt image or to his starring career, which was disappearing almost as rapidly as it had materialized four years before. A 1930 talkie series for Big 4 Productions marked the end of his starring career, but while his days at the top had been brief, Buddy worked well into the sound era in supporting and bit roles.

One Sunday not too long ago, I spent the day sitting in a small screening room located in a West Los Angeles vault. On the screen in front of me, I watched Buddy Roosevelt perform once more in several of the features from his Lester F. Scott Jr. series. Over 40 years had passed since they were filmed, yet when compared

When he turned villain in the thirties, Buddy's moustache made him even more handsome.

to the pictures made by Bob Custer and others, I felt that Buddy's work had stood the test of time much better and I left that evening with the conviction that this long-neglected western personality and his cinematic adventures deserve more recognition than they have received. Should the day arrive when prints of these pictures are made available to the general public, I'm certain that many younger western fans will agree.

★★★

Bob Steele

One of the few western stars whose reputation and standing in the fraternity exceeds his actual accomplishments, Bob Bradbury was seen regularly on the screen for over three decades before the demise of the program western and his own advancing age forced him into the semi-retirement of character roles. The son of Robert North Bradbury, one of the most active action directors of the silent era, Bob made his starring debut with his brother in a 1921 Pathé series which was sold under the unassuming title of *The Bill and Bob Series*, also occasionally referred to as *The Adventures of Bob and Bill*.

This group of short subjects were quasi-educational in nature, with the two Bradbury boys acting as the audience's guide while exploring the great outdoors. Most followed the pattern of *The American Badger*, in which they climbed a mountain, carefully placed a trap in position, showing exactly how it was done, and then walking off-camera. A subtitle cut in to announce that after a few discouraging days, the rest of the picture had been filmed and the camera returned to the badger trap, at which point one strolled up, sniffed at the hole and was caught in the trap. Somehow, it didn't seem too real, but Bill and Bob tied it up anyway and the film was over, having entertained and instructed at the same time.

Bob was only 14 at this time, but he acquired a camera presence which would serve him well over the next few decades; and during the following years, he gained more and varied experience in quite a number of the films his father directed. Sunset's series of historical westerns during the mid-twenties showed a teenager quite at home before the camera and some of his roles (*With Daniel Boone Through the Wilderness, With Sitting Bull at the Spirit Lake Massacre*) were big enough to allow him sufficient freedom of conception and execution for a more than adequate performance.

Beginning with the 1927 season, 20-year old Bob Bradbury made

Bob Steele.

his first starring appearance in an FBO series of westerns (*The Bandit's Son, Drifting Sands, Breed of the Sunsets, The Riding Renegade*) under the name Bob Steele. A small man, Steele did not quite measure up to his adversaries in stature, but more than compensated for this lack of height with his ability to project a strong action-adventure characterization; Bob Steele was probably the best scrapper the silent western ever knew, regardless of size. Fighting with a ferocity larger than life, the boyish hero with the mop of curly hair quickly carved out a following of fans who were only too happy to applaud his exploits, instead of the milquetoast adventures of other western heroes then in vogue.

In addition to his skill in the manly art of self-defense, he was no slouch at riding and the sight of Bob Steele literally throwing himself on a horse and heading out like a streak was always greeted by a breathless gasp from the audience. As a result of his whirlwind-

Although a small man, Steele was no slouch when it came to loving or fighting, as Barbara Luddy found out.

Al St. John, in the days before he grew the beard which marked him as "Fuzzy" St. John, and Bob Steele in an early talkie, Land of the Missing Men.

in-motion image, Bob was able to overcome his small physical size on the screen; few fans ever took note of the careful casting, which retained the time-honored dictum that the hero must stand at least half a head taller than his leading lady.

Initially, Bob was brought to the screen by R-C Pictures, who released through Film Booking Office, but the gradual takeover of its production by FBO in 1928 brought him into the hands of director Wallace W. Fox and writer Frank Howard Clark, who also scripted many of the Tom Tyler series. Robert North Bradbury occasionally filled in for Fox behind the megaphone, with father and son working exceedingly well together. Placing strong emphasis on action, Clark's scripts were slanted heavily in the direction of deep melodrama, so much so that Bob's pictures closely resembled five-reel serials in content and construction.

His best-remembered role from this era, and still a favorite with Bob Steele fans, was an early one, *The Mojave Kid*. Quite representative of the continuous and fast movement that tended to characterize his silent westerns, *The Mojave Kid* cast Steele as

With Thelma Daniels in The Amazing Vagabond

a grown man whose father had disappeared in the desert some 12 years before. Accidentally overhearing a conversation concerning his father and a hidden treasure, Bob eventually appears at the outlaws' hideout, where he discovers two people of great interest to him; the granddaughter of the outlaw leader (with whom he falls in love) and his father, a captive but still alive and well.

Captured by the outlaws, Bob is flogged in front of his father in an effort to loosen the old man's tongue, which for 12 years has refused to tell the treasure's location (lesser bandits would have killed him long before and got on with the serious business of outlawing). But Steele gets away and holds off the gang until a solution is agreed upon—he is to fight one of the band for his freedom, and that of the girl and his father. Although briefly a tossup, Bob wins hands down in a brutal brawl and the party takes its leave, only to have the gang revolt against their leader. Hot on Bob's heels in pursuit, the renegades receive their just reward in the form of a dynamite explosion on the trail, set by their deposed leader, who turns out to be a man of honor after all and one who keeps his word, even though it kills him in the process. Three

Bob and Lola Mendez in Headin' for Danger

outlaws escape the explosion but Steele disposes of them to wrap up the picture with a wedding and reunion. Although not too terribly logical in many places and filled with questionable motivation throughout, no sagebrush fan could deny the excitement generated by this little ball of liquid lightning and even though he temporarily deserted the West for part of 1928–29 (*Come and Get It, Heading for Danger*), his fans remained loyal.

Bob made the transition to sound with a low-pitched voice containing just the hint of a burr or rasp in his speech. This worked in his favor, offsetting his small size and youthful appearance by strengthening the virility of his screen image. While he made an enormous quantity of films for Monogram, Republic and many independents during the thirties and forties, Bob Steele, like Tom Tyler and Ken Maynard, never quite made it into the ranks of the top western stars of the sound era, but his cinematic adventures were usually worth watching and whiled away many pleasant Saturday afternoons for matinee audiences.

Bob came out of the obscurity of quasi-retirement to delight his fans with a solid performance as Trooper Duffy in television's *F Troop* series until it left the air and now spends his time doing that which he loves best—playing a pretty fair round of golf and enjoying the California sunshine. Life is no longer a short interval between pictures, and truthfully he's kind of glad it turned out this way.

Roy Stewart

Roy Stewart came to the screen with Majestic in 1913, and before his career ended he could claim the distinction of having worked for just about every motion picture company that counted—and some that didn't. A native of San Diego, Stewart had toured the West Coast for several years in traveling stock companies before joining the ranks of the "canned drama" producers, and although he was a reasonably competent actor who could play dramatic leads as well as light comedy (he once worked briefly for Hal Roach at the very outset of Roach's production career), Roy's career did not progress very rapidly until he joined Triangle in 1916.

William S. Hart had saddled up his mount for the last time and his move over to the Paramount banner had left a wide gap in the Triangle release schedule. Hoping to offset the loss, H. O. Davis, Triangle general manager, cast the rugged Stewart (with whom he had worked at Universal earlier) in a series of western roles. Roy caught on with fans as the Triangle stage stars had never been able to, and within a few months he had surfaced as one of Triangle's three big guns at the box-office. As luck would have it, the company soon collapsed but Roy had made his reputation in time, and when the end came he was prepared to move on.

Smoothly paced with snappy action and few dull moments, his Triangle features were directed for the most part by Cliff Smith, who was developing a surefire touch that would make its presence well-known in the westerns of the mid-twenties. While there was little originality in Alvin J. Neitz's scripts, there was plenty of action and melodrama, which greatly pleased fans to whom the "high-brow" Triangle pictures of earlier days had been but a bore.

After leaving Triangle, Roy appeared in numerous society dramas for Goldwyn and Selznick but his big roles were in Benjamin B. Hampton's *The U.P. Trail* in 1920 and Quality Films' *The Heart of the North* in 1921. This latter feature presented Roy in a dual role, as a RCNW Mountie and his outlaw brother. While the

Roy Stewart.

"mistaken identity" plot had been used countless times before, Stewart made his lawman an impressive character and the outlaw a thoroughly despicable one, without exaggerating his acting. The climax was truly a western fan's delight—the brothers met in the forest during a raging thunderstorm. As the Mountie did not relish killing his brother, he found himself facing a loaded gun held by a hand not bothered by such pangs of conscience. But just as Roy (the Mountie) was about to be done in by Roy (the outlaw), a

Stewart made many non-western dramatic appearances early in his career.

His initial films for Triangle were straight dramatic roles, but H. O. Davis saw him as Bill Hart's replacement in 1917.

Roy Stewart presented an awesome appearance in his Triangle westerns. These quickly placed him as one of Triangle's top three box-office attractions in 1917.

bolt of lightning came to the rescue, toppling a tree over the villain and preserving the "always-gets-his-man" theme.

This particular film led to a contract with Ben Wilson to make a western series for Arrow release and while he concentrated mainly on western roles from this point on, Stewart was one of the few western stars adept enough to move back and forth between western and non-western roles without adversely affecting his career. His contract with Arrow resulted in some strong westerns (*Back to Yellow Jacket, One-Eighth Apache*) and was followed by work at Principal (*Riding Wild, The Sagebrush Trail*) and then back to Universal, where Roy worked overtime turning out features, several quick groups of western shorts (*Timber Tales, The Lumberjack* series) and one serial, *The Radio King*. One of the busiest of the western actors during the early twenties, he managed to sandwich several films for Western Pictures Exploitation and FBO in between his other work.

But what turned out to be his best remembered roles were done for Anthony J. Xydias's Sunset Productions in a scattering of romanticized historical westerns, many of which are still available today. Playing the leading (but not always the title) roles in films like *Buffalo Bill on The U.P. Trail, With General Custer at the Little Big Horn* and *With Kit Carson Over the Great Divide,* Roy turned in some good acting performances. While these pictures were marred to some extent by the padding of the ever-present and inevitable romantic sequences, and by some overly melodramatic acting by the rest of the casts, most turned out to be solid portrayals on Stewart's part. One of the better features in this group, *With Daniel Boone Through the Wilderness* remained quite faithful to

The Learnin' of Jim Benton *was one of Roy's strongest Triangle films.*

"Trust me, I didn't do it." From **The Learnin' of Jim Benton.**

the popular conception of the backwoods hero, but Stewart was occasionally able to inject a breath of the rigors of frontier life in colonial America. Only George O'Brien, in his 1936 *Daniel Boone*, ever brought more realism to the portrayal of Boone, although Fess Parker and television have certainly made Kentucky's #1 citizen far more popular.

Strong supporting casts, which often included a youthful Bob Bradbury, Jack Mower, Earle Metcalf and Henry B. Walthall, and the direction of Robert North Bradbury helped to make these Sunset westerns a fairly strong independent series. Unfortunately, some were badly weakened by the inability or unwillingness of Sunset to spend sufficient money warranted by the story and while the first four or five reels held the audience interest, the dismal climax had all the earmarks of a production crew that had suddenly discovered its script writer was on a weekend binge with the rest of the company funds. After building up for a smashing finish, the story ended with a whimper—the big battle or showdown never materialized, or else our hero rode off into the sunset, leaving the rest of the cast to cope with the problem in a kind of open ending. But most held up well from beginning to end, and when viewed today beside representative selections from the majority of other inde-

Kathleen Williams and Roy in Benjamin B. Hampton's The U. P. Trail.

Stewart's contract with Ben Wilson produced some good independent westerns. A scene from Back to Yellow Jacket *with Kathleen Kirkham.*

Roy was not above hitting his leading lady now and then, if the occasion warranted it.

Roy in one of his Lumberjack series.

Esther Ralston and Roy in Tall Timber, *a 1923 Universal two-reeler.*

Roy's career ended with his death in 1933.

pendent series of the time (Syndicate, Truart, Pizor, etc.), show a good deal of ingenuity and production value by comparison.

Surviving the crisis of sound, Roy continued to be very active before the camera until his death in 1933. A likeable fellow with more talent than many of his contemporaries, Stewart was well thought of by co-workers and while he never reached the rarified atmosphere of top stardom, his name was a sight welcomed by exhibitors in small towns across the nation. A Roy Stewart feature was an excellent compromise between the high-priced Mix, Gibson and Jones films and their usual fare of independent westerns, for few theatres could ever complain that Roy's pictures failed to make them money. Unfortunately, all that seems to remain of Roy's career today are a few of the Sunset features and Universal short subjects (many of which are found in the possession of English collectors), hardly a representative selection of the man's work. Celluloid fame is a very fragile thing.

Fred Thomson

From the standpoint of popularity and financial earnings, the silent western's most popular star behind William S. Hart and Tom Mix was an ex-minister named Fred Thomson. In a starring career that lasted just about six years, Thomson earned an estimated $2.5 million; Buck Jones and Ken Maynard each appeared in leading roles for two decades and their estimated earnings were only slightly higher, $3 million. Thomson had left the ministry after World War I to enter pictures, a move he later attributed to the ability of the screen to reach millions of people, especially youngsters, with a message of clean living. Within two years, the boy from nearby Pasadena would ride the skyrocket from Poverty Row quickies to fame and fortune, delivering his ideals in a palatable form as he went.

There is no doubt that Hollywood was sorely in need of a new image at the time; the unsolved murder of William Desmond Taylor, the drug-induced death of Wallace Reid and the sordid accusations against popular comic Roscoe Arbuckle had exposed the tinsel town as an early-day Peyton Place and a nation just emerging from the Victorian era was shocked by the stories of the dissolution and dissipation in which their favorites indulged, and probably harbored strong resentments at their own dull, drab lives.

Fred's first noteworthy appearance was in Universal's *The Eagle's Talons*, a 1923 serial, but Universal seemed a dead end and he signed with Monogram (a small independent bearing no relation to the Monogram of the thirties) for a series of six feature westerns (*The Sheriff of Tombstone, North of Nevada, The Mask of Lopez*), to be released through Film Booking Office. Monogram R-C Pictures and FBO all had a hand in the series, but the one consistent factor was H. J. Brown Productions.

Harry Joe Brown, who would also guide the destinies of Ken Maynard to fame, was responsible for the early Thomson westerns, and with Al Rogell directing from scripts by Marion Jackson, this

Fred Thomson.

trio quickly placed Fred in the forefront of the western ranks. But Thomson was not just another stick figure molded to heroic proportions by press agents; he was a talented personality whose youthful appearance hid any hint of the popularity to come. A somewhat bashful and retiring sort, Fred possessed a fine athletic build and sense of timing, a facility for light comedy and enough spunk to do his own stunts without benefit of a double. His pictures were designed to appeal to the youth of America and Fred maintained the same high moral standards off the screen that he por-

A scene from Chapter 11 of Fred's 1923 Universal serial, The Eagle's Talons.

*A frame enlargement from one of the Monogram westerns that brought Fred Thomson to the attention of FBO—*The Mask of Lopez *with David Kirby.*

Many of Fred's westerns had a 'South of the Border' motif and involved lovely senoritas, as in Hands Across The Border . . .

And Don Mike.

Fred learns that his best friend was responsible for his father's death in this scene from **The Two Gun Man.**

trayed on it; there were no rumors or scandals connected with Thomson's private life.

His FBO westerns were carefully constructed, with the romantic element well balanced with thrill sequences and rapidly paced throughout—a reasonably good mixture of sentiment, humor and adventure mixed together and served up in a frothy, if sometimes illogical, blend which immediately won him the allegiance of western and non-western fans alike. And if they were looking for a moral, Fred gave it to them, as in *The Two Gun Man,* in which he demonstrated that one's ends could be as easily reached without resorting to violence, even though the quicker way was sorely tempting at times.

Playing the veteran returning from the war, Fred found his dad's homestead had been mortgaged and the cattle stolen. Learning that his trusted friend was behind the attempt to steal the ranch after his dad died, Fred strapped on his guns to settle the affair as he would have in the Army. But Olive Hasbrouck dissuaded him from more killing and Thomson resorted to a more subtle approach.

Fred went to work for his villainous friend, and using both his gun and his head, regained his cattle, picked up a reward for the rustler, saved the kidnapped Olive and lured the outlaw gang

Fred mixed sentiment, light comedy and action in films like Lone Hand Saunders.

Fred usually managed a confession without the use of gunplay, as in Ridin' the Wind.

Imaginative photography such as this low-level shot made Jesse James *a strong performer at the box-office.*

into the sheriff's hands—all in six reels. Of course, there were a few improbable situations, such as overcoming half a dozen men in a brawl that took place within the confines of a small room, but for a man whose horse could bury a body and neatly place a wreath and cross on the finished gravesite before leaving to join his master (*Thundering Hoofs*—Silver King was reputed to be a retired veteran of the Los Angeles Fire Department when Fred acquired him), nothing was really impossible and *The Two Gun Man* became one of the few series westerns to play first-run houses on Broadway, opening at the Warner Theatre in July 1926.

With the immense following which Fred had acquired so quickly, there was every reason to expect that Thomson would be approached by larger producers, and true to form Adolph Zukor and Paramount won the bidding game. Happily married to screen writer Frances Marion, who had given Fred his break in *Just Around the Corner,* her 1921 Cosmopolitan picture, Thomson left FBO and made a number of extravagantly mounted features (*Jesse

The Sunset Legion.

James, Kit Carson, The Pioneer Scout, The Sunset Legion) for Paramount.

Just how valuable an attraction he proved to be is pointed up by the box-office gross of *Jesse James*, which brought over $1.2 million into the Paramount coffers. A glamorization of the outlaw's life, *Jesse James* opened with some spectacular Civil War scenes, but not a single bank robbery was shown and the film came to a rather abrupt ending when Jesse was shot to death—the only one of Fred's pictures in which he died at the end.

Directed by Lloyd Ingraham, the Thomson Paramounts were longer than his FBO westerns—six to eight reels—and more slowly and deliberately paced, with a stronger element of logic in Frank Clifton's stories. All held up well at the box-office and Fred was in the process of surpassing Mix (Hart had retired in 1925) when he was suddenly taken ill and died of pneumonia in 1928. The fastest-rising potential on the western scene had been removed as quickly as he appeared.

Few of the Fred Thomson westerns are in circulation today, but those that are give us some insight into the rapid rise of this western star whose appeal went beyond western fans to touch

With comic Charlie Murray in The Pioneer Scout.

Kit Carson

general audiences. While his films presented the same superficial and distorted picture of the West with which fans had become comfortable in the twenties, Fred's starring vehicles differed in that they were sophisticated and highly polished specimens, and with his lively personality filled a void on the screen. Entertainment was prerequisite to success in the western genre and Fred Thomson gave of himself in sufficient quantity—yet so did Yakima Canutt in his FBO films, and while both performed dangerous, tricky stunts and engaged in effortless acrobatics, Yak failed to achieve anything close to the popularity Fred attained. Somewhere, the chemistry of stardom also differed and Fred Thomson possessed the winning element in plentiful quantity. Had Thomson lived another decade, Mix probably would have surrendered his crown much earlier to the luminary whose career ended with his star still very much in the ascent.

★★★

Tom Tyler

Vincent Markowski was not at all impressive at first sight; certainly his appearance did not reveal the fact that this Port Henry, New York, boy was a champion weight lifter and strongman. Unlike Joe Bonomo (who billed himself as "The World's Perfect Man"), Lucien Albertini and other strongmen of the day, Markowski's lean, lithe body gracefully concealed the fact that he was a muscle-man. Reaching Hollywood in 1924, young Markowski was determined to swap his weights for an acting career, and once he took off his shirt to flex his muscles a few times Vince had no difficulty in finding work as an extra.

But his ambitions ran higher and as soon as he could afford one, Markowski armed himself with a portfolio of suitable photographs and began making the rounds of studio casting offices. His investment eventually brought Vince a sizeable role in M-G-M's *The Only Thing*, and when filming was completed on this picture, it was back to the casting offices for the thespian who could now boast of solid acting experience before the camera. FBO, one of the foremost exponents of the western genre in the twenties, was in the market for a new series and Markowski discovered that the only thing separating him from leading roles at R-C Pictures, who released through FBO, was the answer to one simple question, "Can you ride a horse?"

Without hesitation, Vince replied in the affirmative, shook hands on the proposition and went out to find someone who could make him an accomplished horseman in one week. By the time shooting began, few suspected that only a few days before, their leading man had not known the right side of a horse from its left. When *Let's Go Gallagher* was released in October 1925, reviewers commented on his fine riding ability and predicted a marked success for the new star.

And so fame fell about the shoulders of 22-year old Vincent Markowski in the form of instant stardom and a new name—Tom

Tom Tyler.

Tyler. A likeable hero with a low-key personality on-screen, Tom held his own with the other FBO cowboy stars and shortly began to surpass them at the box-office. His riding grew better with each film and the screen brawling required in each picture came naturally to the athletically inclined actor. The Tyler style of acting was relaxation, so much so that many were convinced he couldn't act. And here was another handsome hero in the same vein as Jack

Little Frankie Darro was a big hit as Tom's sidekick in films like **The Masquerade Bandit.**

Perrin—was he to face career restrictions similar to those which had limited Perrin's stardom? Not exactly, for while virtue was considered a manly attribute of the western formula hero in the twenties, Tom Tyler often stepped outside this boundary to play the badman, redeemed by love of the heroine of the efforts of a small boy. Tom's portrayals were varied just enough to keep him from becoming as stereotyped with fans as had Perrin. Jack's halo was brand-new in every one of his pictures; occasionally Tom couldn't find his.

Tom also had the good fortune of acquiring a production unit that respected him and worked together as a team to make the FBO Tyler westerns as good as possible. Robert De Lacy directed, with Frank Howard Clark scripting and Nick Musuraca photographing most of Tom's pictures. Supporting casts were up to par and the inclusion of nine-year old Frankie Darro in the early Tyler westerns proved an immediate hit with fans. Intensely interested in following Tom's footsteps to the top as an actor, Darro gave excellent performances which eventually carried him to a brief stardom in the thirties. At the same time, his presence gave Tom a sidekick, providing the writers with plot motivation as well as a guaranteed

The Sonora Kid.

'Tell the truth, now.' Tom and Frankie in The Arizona Streak.

Tom stepped out of western garb in The Cowboy Cop.

Tom Tyler's athletic background made him a natural for realistic screen fights.

"out" for any predicament in which they might place the hero. This team approach worked well, and when Frankie was not saving Tom from some dastardly plot, it was usually because he had been kidnapped, giving Tom a chance to return the favor.

Many of Tom's FBO westerns were imaginative scripted and appropriately titled—*Wyoming Wildcat, The Sonora Kid, Phantom of the Range, The Avenging Rider*—and not all of them were strictly westerns in the accepted vein; he stepped outside the line with *The Cowboy Cop* and *Tom and His Pals*, but an unbroken string of features carried Tom Tyler into 1929 and the end of FBO. Syndicate Pictures signed Tom and several of the other FBO stars for a 1929–30 series, and as might be expected the quality of these independent oaters was several notches below his FBO films. Long shots were extensively utilized, apparently for reasons of economy, and Tom was given little to do for most of each picture. *The Canyon of Missing Men* was typical, with Tom playing a member of J. P. McGowan's band (you guessed it, J. P. also directed) of rustlers who spurned bandit queen Sheila LeGay's affections for those of Arden Ellis, whose rancher father was being driven out of business

Born to Battle, *and it looks as if that's exactly what Tom intends to do.*

Even a hero is human. Tom is just about to discover that his adversary not only has the drop on The Cowboy Musketeer, *but also holds the upper hand. Ten more seconds and Tom will strong-arm him into submission.*

by the outlaws. This and his other Syndicate films were uniformly but slowly paced and failed to generate the excitement usually associated with Tom Tyler's screen work.

While waiting for Syndicate to equip for sound production in late 1930, Tom made *Phantom of the West* for Mascot release, proving his voice was satisfactory for talkies. Returning to Syndicate (which, as its name suggests, was really an association of smaller independent showmen like J. Charles Davis II and Robert J. Horner) in early 1931, Tom began the second phase of a career that would see him star in 43 feature westerns and four more serials before leaving the screen briefly in 1938 to tour with the Wallace Brothers Circus. The choice role as Luke Plummer, John Wayne's antagonist in *Stagecoach* marked his return in 1939 and signaled the beginning of a long series of unusual characterizations, but it was his work in *The Mummy's Hand* and two serials, *The Adventures of Captain Marvel* and *The Phantom*, which endeared him most to the matinee audiences of the forties.

Although never quite rising into the ranks of the top western

Tyler made a large number of independent westerns in the thirties. By 1935 and Reliable's Born to Battle, *Tom had lost his boyish appearance and made a handsome, mature leading man.*

stars, Tom Tyler continued making westerns until late in the forties, when arthritis gradually forced his retirement from the screen. Returning to his sister's home in Detroit, Tom also had to bow out of a proposed television series, while watching his once-muscular physique and fine sense of timing destroyed by a crippling disease. Death mercifully came to Tom Tyler of a heart attack on May 1, 1954 at the age of 50. Although his screen career had been lengthy and filled with a variety of roles and fine performances, Tom Tyler wanted to be remembered for his western portrayals and his fans agreed—this was as it should be.

★★

Wally Wales

(THE COWBOY PRINCE)

Lester F. Scott's early success with his Buddy Roosevelt and Buffalo Bill Jr. series spelled stardom for still another unknown, Floyd T. Alderson. A native of Wyoming, Alderson's background was very similar to that of Roosevelt and Jay Wilsey; a real-life cowpuncher, he entered pictures around 1914 and labored in obscurity for years. By the time Scott brought him to the screen as Wally Wales, Alderson had more than a decade of experience in a career that had stubbornly refused to budge beyond bit parts and stunt doubling.

A serious young man, Alderson was intent on making the most of his long-awaited opportunity and he worked hard to make his mark. Looking back today, it seems a bit ludicrous to find that Wally Wales was a star earning only $500 a picture (Roosevelt and Wilsey started at the same price and never earned much more on Scott's payroll), but the Scott westerns were inexpensively made. Cameraman Ray Ries recalls that he received $250 per picture and that supporting cast members were paid as little as possible, allowing Scott to bring in his pictures for a paltry $10,000–15,000 each. The expenditure of $20,000 represented a very special picture and was an occasion reserved mainly for the days of Pathé releases. Exteriors were shot at the Iverson Ranch, a favorite site with independent producers, and interiors in rented studio space wherever it happened to be available. Long hours and night work were not uncommon to the production of Action Pictures and with no guilds or unions to interfere, Scott was able to get the most for his small investment.

When the decision was made to expand Action Pictures' output in late 1924, both Scott and Louis Weiss surveyed the available actors, and hired Alderson. The next problem was his name—Floyd T. Anderson was not exactly a box-office magnet as it stood. Betty Burbridge recalls that they were looking over his publicity portfolio

The Cowboy Prince.

before Alderson arrived on the lot. Someone remarked that he resembled the then-Prince of Wales and suggested Neddy Wales as a screen name. The session ended with Wally Wales as the agreed-upon name change, and billed as "The Cowboy Prince," Wally had a decided advantage over his fellow cowpokes on the Action lot—he came across on-screen as an extremely youthful appearing, handsome hero with a flair for light comedy. His scripts by Miss Burbridge and Richard Thorpe (writing under the pseudonym of Frank L. Inghram) were fashioned around this quiet,

Fannie Midgley, Wally and Jean Arthur, in the days before she became a blonde.

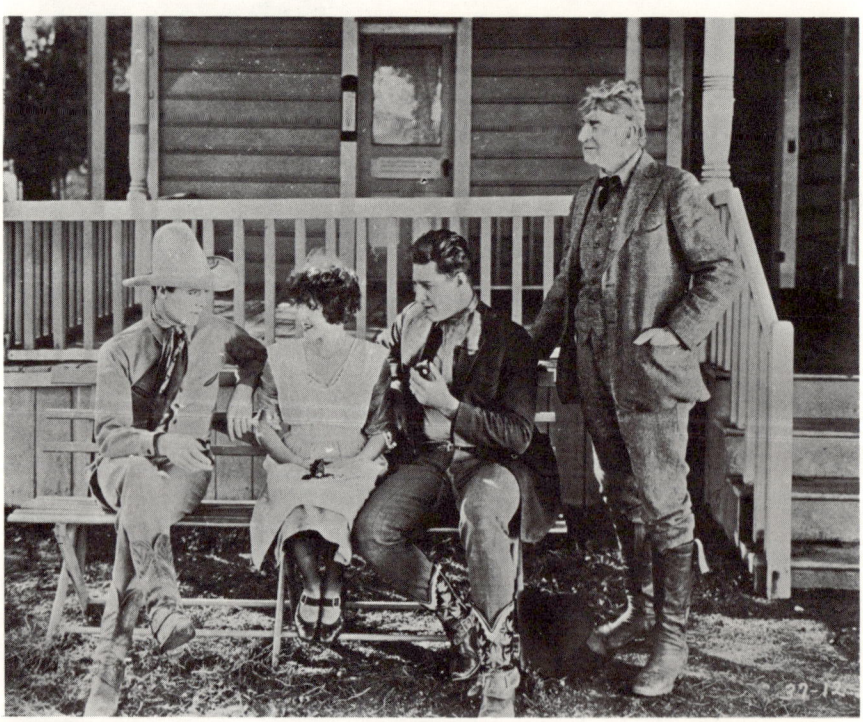

Wally, Jean Arthur and Frank Ellis discuss their next Action picture.

Frank Ellis and Jean Arthur care for the wounded Wally.

Jean and Wally return the favor a few reels later.

Frank Ellis and Wally Wales.

reserved personality with the deceptive comic touch. While the Jay Wilsey features were rather light-hearted affairs with a somewhat heavy-handed but gregarious hero, Wally's pictures usually began on a comic note, only to switch rapidly to the serious. This presented the unsuspecting viewer with a change of pace and relaxed him for the rip-snorting antics of a stunt athlete whose intense fighting and riding scenes were offset by his romantic interludes. A refined hero, his pictures inevitably contained a scene in which the grimly determined young man always seemed to be saying goodbye for the first time to a mother figure.

Tearin' Loose, Wally's first Action Picture, was released in June 1925 and set the stage for the characterization that his writers would develop. Insisting upon a strange silence that caused our tight-lipped hero to be jailed at one point in the film, and suspected of attempted burglary at another, Wally was faced with the problem of unmasking the villain and his sister, who were posing as relatives of a wealthy rancher. In doing so, Wally won the girl's love and revealed himself as the one being impersonated.

Carefully constructed to gain audience sympathy at the opening

Frank Ellis, Jean Arthur, Alma Bennett and Wally.

of each film, Wally's roles were dimensional and vigorous. *Twisted Triggers* found Wally and Jean Arthur as good friends, their fathers as mortal enemies. After one of their periodic quarrels, Jean's father was found dead and Wally's dad was accused of the murder. A young criminal befriended earlier by Wally suspected a frame-up and rejoined his old gang to pass our hero the evidence he needed to clear his father and clean up the range. In *The Soda Water Cowboy*, Wally was a sickly young man sent West on his doctor's orders to rest and ended up with Beryl Roberts on his arm and a badge on his chest.

Wally Wales fans were always prepared for the unusual, but *White Pebbles* caught them completely off-guard. Olive Hasbrouck's cattle were being rustled when Wally made his appearance as a tenderfoot in need of a job. A rash of murders took place as her ranch hands were gunned down one by one and everything pointed to the foreman as the chief suspect. Kids accustomed to the serials of the twenties had no difficulty in determining that the foreman was innocent but the denouement caught them as flat-footed as the adult members of the audience—the foreman was indeed innocent,

A scene from White Pebbles, *one of the most unusual western plots ever to appear on the silent screen.*

Frank Ellis and Wally consider the badge offered them by Whitehorse.

Wally comforts Fannie Midgley in a scene which was standard in many of his Action Pictures. From Ridin' Rivals.

he just looked and acted guilty. The ranch hands themselves were the rustlers, and each time cattle turned up missing the Chinese cook, whose devotion went beyond the call of duty, killed one of them in repayment.

With plots like these and the capable direction of Dick Thorpe, it is little wonder that Scott's Action Pictures stood head and shoulders above Sunset, Anchor and other independents. Wally also had the good fortune to work with a competent supporting cast, some of whom (Walter Brennan, Boris Karloff and Jean Arthur, most notably) would work a good deal more mileage from their careers than he was able to. Harry Todd, whose career dated back to Essanay and the days of Broncho Billy Anderson, carved a new niche for himself, providing the comic relief for Wally, as well as for Buddy and Jay on occasions.

Wally's starring career followed a pattern similar to Scott's other stars; following Pathé cancellation of his series, Wally played a few leading roles, including a 10-episode Ben Wilson serial with Jean Delores (*The Voice From The Sky*, 1929) and a role in Leo Maloney's *Overland Bound*, then fell into supporting

Wally in an early talkie role, still frowning upon wine, women and song. Riders of the Cactus.

parts. Changing his name to Hal Taliaferro, he turned villain in the late thirties. His most important role came when he was cast as Bob Stuart in Republic's 1938 serial, *The Lone Ranger*. One of the five actors presented to the audience in the first chapter as suspected of being the masked man, he had the misfortune to be killed off rather early. Had Wally's part been a more substantial one, he might well have met with the same success which two of the others (Bruce Bennett and George Montgomery) enjoyed. But *The Lone Ranger* failed to revive his starring career and Wally, now Hal, went back to playing villains.

Unlike a number of the western stars, Wally had the foresight to protect his financial interests and when television shot a large hole in the movie business during the early fifties, and work for the old-timers grew scarce, he left Hollywood to return home. He had taken care to retain his interest in the family ranch, and at this writing he still puts in a full day riding the range. Of Lester F. Scott's three stars, Floyd T. Alderson made the most of his career. Unfortunately, his Action Pictures have disappeared from sight. Neither the major archives nor private collectors, to my knowledge, possess them, and the few that do remain rest in a

In the mid-thirties, Wally changed his name to Hal Taliaferro and became a villain.

tightly sealed vault in West Los Angeles. While their owner has explored the possibility of making some available to collectors, the financial return is insufficient to interest him and so another page in sagebrush history is slowly deteriorating, to disappear completely one day, along with the fading memories of "The Cowboy Prince." I feel it a stroke of good fortune that my memories are recent ones.

★★

Ted Wells

While the potential of western stardom had been wide open during the silent era, the distant rumblings of sound over the screen's horizon caused producers to shut the gates as early as 1926. Although a few personalities were allowed to join the select group of aspirants after that date, not one had sufficient time or opportunity to build the necessary audience following, and as a result found themselves doomed to obscurity in spite of their best efforts.

One such was a handsome rodeo performer from Texas named Ted Wells. Coming to the screen in the fall of 1927 under the Universal banner, Wells's first appearance was in *Straight Shooting*, directed by William Wyler, who had graduated from short subjects to feature direction. Wells was a whale of a rider, whose fistic abilities and knack with a gun made him a natural for western heroism on the screen, but in his bid for stardom, Ted was fighting a battle with odds he couldn't possibly overcome, though he could hardly be expected to know that the finger of Fate had marked him for but a brief public view, just as it would the career of Lane Chandler.

The story of a valuable gold mine owned by an oldtimer and his double-crossing nephew, *Straight Shooting* made an impressive debut for Wells. The nephew was out to do his uncle in for his own foul purposes, but Ted appeared in town to save both the mine and its owner from the machinations of Joe Bennett, winning Lillian Gilmore's hand in the process. Only slightly over four reels in length, this unpretentious but good little western brought praise from hard-nosed reviewers, and with today's emphasis on the director's importance in a film's success, the fact that Wyler directed it would be the automatic explanation for its acceptance, but one should not overlook William Lester's scripting, nor the contribution of Ted and the rest of the cast. With the exception of *The Thunder Riders*, his westerns invariably were well-accepted. Interestingly enough, Wyler also directed this one, but from Carl Krusada's script. Enough said.

Ted Wells.

With a choice lot of Universal's youthful leading ladies supporting his heroic efforts, Ted Wells worked into late 1929 for Universal, saving ranches, mining properties, and other assorted assets for the likes of Kathleen Collins (*Gun Grit, The Riding Demon*), Duane Thompson (*Born to the Saddle, Bravery and Bullets*), Kathryn McGuire (*Border Wildcat*), Derelys Perdue (*Smiling Terror*) and Lillian Gilmore. With two seasons of screen exposure to his credit, Ted Wells would have been ready to strike out in a definite direction to consolidate his experience and form his image into a lasting one, but it was all over for him. Building the foundation had been to no avail, for Universal's western production was cut back and reorganized during 1930, with none but the leading sagebrush stars like Ken Maynard held under contract

Rodeo champion Ted was better remembered for his portrayals in the Pawnee Bill Jr. *series made by Bob Horner.*

—proven box-office performers whose identity and following were well established.

Ted Wells is virtually forgotten today, but his alter ego is firmly implanted in the memory of every western aficionado who ever attended Saturday matinees with any regularity, for through the belated courtesy of Robert J. Horner and his Associated Independent Productions, Ted appeared on the screen in 1928 under the guise of one Pawnee Bill Jr. in a series of eight westerns. Operating from P.O. Box 32, Associated Independent offered exhibitors such exciting titles as *Across the Plains, Cheyenne Trails, The Mystery Rider,*

Straight Shootin'

Ted's good looks made it difficult for him to appear mean and rough, but the six-shooter in his hand was pretty convincing. From The Crimson Canyon.

As Betty Caldwell's foreman, Ted exposed a crooked lawyer as the head of a rustling ring in **Greased Lightning,** *1927.*

The Thrill Chaser, Arizona Speed, Forbidden Trails, The Texas Flash and *Where the West Begins.* Written and directed by Horner, these independent westerns were made in 1927 before Ted's association with Universal began, but Horner, whose presence in the industry in the late twenties varied with his financial resources, was too broke to market the films until the following year. The series sat in limbo, and was not released until 1928.

The Pawnee Bill Jr., series was not a very good one; in fact,

The Border Wildcat.

it was a terrible group of poorly made films which gave Ted all the appearance of being nothing more than another drugstore cowboy. Had they been exhibited in other than the small town theatres, these pictures could have destroyed the box-office potential of his Universal westerns with ease. And yet, while Ted Wells is forgotten today, Pawnee Bill Jr. is remembered with a tenacity that denies rational explanation, other than the glory associated with the original owner of the name. It's a topsy-turvy world sometimes, where mediocrity replaces quality with an acceptance difficult to understand, but even though Ted Wells failed in his bid for sagebrush stardom and has been forgotten he's still remembered today.

Guinn "Big Boy" Williams

He wandered out of Texas during World War I, a tall, lanky cowboy bearing the unlikely name of Guinn Williams. With a perennial appearance wavering between homespun bashfulness and the quizzical wonderment of a country boy left to the wiles of the big city, he landed in Hollywood in 1918 as "Tex" Williams and set out to make his fortune in front of the movie cameras. His bid for stardom never quite gathered sufficient steam, but Guinn did succeed in becoming one of the best-known western character actors and enjoyed a screen career that lasted nearly four decades.

Williams's first role brought him a new name and a friendship of which he always remained proud. Playing a small role in a Goldwyn feature of 1919, *Almost a Husband*, Guinn was introduced to humorist Will Rogers. Delivered with the famous infectious smile, Rogers's greeting was short and simple, "My, you're a big boy!" After a moment's deliberation, Will announced that from then on Guinn was to be known as Big Boy. Professing a distaste for the fact that every cowboy he met in the movie capital went by the name "Tex," the Oklahoma comic had decided that it was about time someone started a new trend in cowboy names and Williams might as well lead the way. Delighted with the attention paid to him by Will, and wise enough to realize the publicity value inherent in being nicknamed by the fast-rising country philosopher, "Tex" became Big Boy Williams.

Only 22 years old, Big Boy's first starring roles came his way in the form of a 1921 contract with Charles R. Seeling, and *The Jack Riders*, his first feature released by Aywon in September, was greeted with praise. A comic western with a touch of melodrama, it had practically no story at all, but that didn't really matter; few of the independent westerns of that period could boast of a strong, logical story anyway. What was really important was the appearance of a fresh new personality and Big Boy was just that.

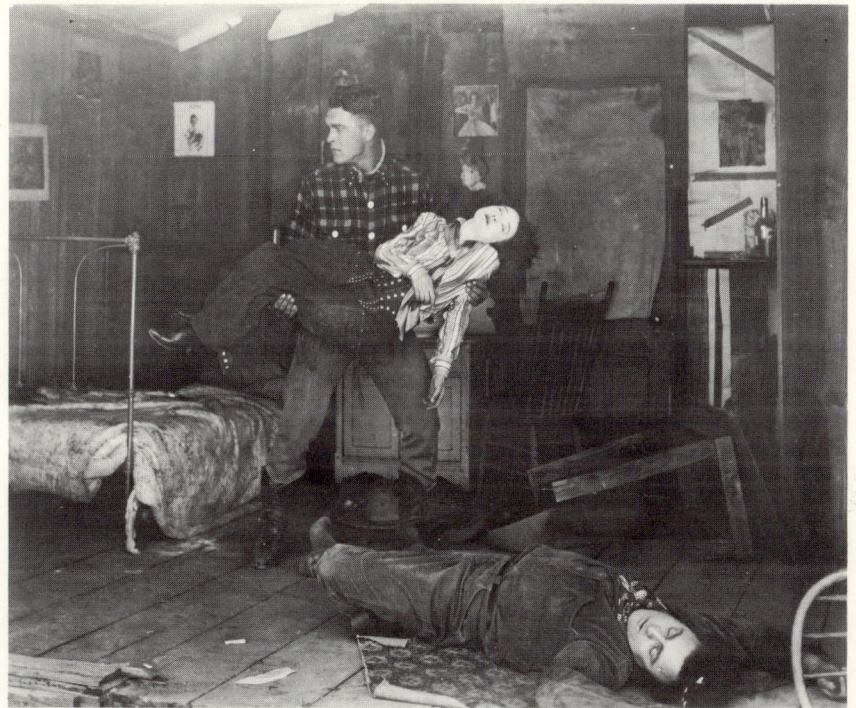

Big Boy in **Across the Border,** *1924.*

The Jack Riders concerned a young tenderfoot whose inheritance of his father's ranch was conditional on his coming West to prove his manhood. If he should not be equal to the occasion, the ranch was to immediately revert to the villain, who held the mortgage. Of course, the villain created all sorts of embarrassing moments for our hero, right up until the end when Big Boy won a rodeo contest, paid off the mortgage and married the banker's daughter. With this as a theme, the door was left wide open for comedy, for which Williams showed a keen talent; his first contact with a bucking bronc reduced Big Boy to riding a donkey around town until the very end of the picture, an ignominious fate for a would-be hero, but appropriate to the role and well done by Williams, whose blissful unawareness of the incongruity added to the humor.

Cast in the role of Big Boy's sidekick, little Will Rogers Jr. made Williams work hard to keep ahead. Youngsters are the best scene-stealers in the business and young Rogers proved himself a chip off the old block when it came to riding and roping. His presence in Big Boy's Aywon westerns added a touch of human interest in much the same way that Buzz Barton would give a big boost to the Jack Perrin Rayart westerns in the mid-twenties.

The remainder of this series was equally interesting, at least in story synopsis; I've never come across prints of the other films but if the trade reviewers are to be believed, Big Boy had all the necessary potential for solid stardom. His skill at riding, shooting and fighting was unquestioned and the enthusiasm he put into each portrayal came across in a genuine manner.

But there's a fine line between a good character actor and a mediocre star—it may be talent or the properties in which the actor works, it can even be the company for which he works or the press agent who works for him. Western actors were a dime a dozen in the early twenties; director George Marshall once observed that shaking any tree in the vicinity of Hollywood would bring a shower of cowboys, ready and willing to go to work. Guinn's next contract would assure him of permanent obscurity; he signed a three-year pact in early 1922 with Frederich Herbst Productions. The half-dozen five-reelers called for each season were directed by W. Hughes

Big Boy's silent westerns were rough and tumble affairs. This scene is from **The Black Cyclone,** *1926.*

Curran and the finished films distributed to the independent market by DiLorenzo, Inc.

That the Herbst films (*Blaze Away, Trail of Hate*) were good entertainment was mainly due to Big Boy's presence, for the stories were next to nothing and production values nonexistent. While Williams stood out far and above the material with which he had to work, he never had a chance to beat the system. One independent film led to another. There was no opportunity for publicity with these obscure production companies and hardly a chance to build a real following of fans. With no consistent booking policy (exchanges bought the films in groups, but exhibitors often exercised an option to pick and choose), and the fierce competition that raged on the state-right market before overproduction caused the slump of 1922, it was every press agent for himself and Big Boy remained at the bottom of the heap.

When Herbst went bankrupt, Williams moved back over to Nathan Hirsh's Aywon for his final starring series (*Rounding Up the Law, Cyclone Jones, End of the Rope*), a group of fairly polished independent westerns considering the budgets. Big Boy's famed squint was now fully developed, giving him the appearance of a huge grizzly bear about to throw a tantrum. This further enhanced his unusual screen personality—still a refreshing change from that projected by a majority of the pseudo-cowboys of the period.

About this same time, he had moved into supporting roles, playing the heavy in William Fairbanks's Arrow westerns in order to make ends meet. His starring roles had paid only $250 a picture; and a fellow his size had to eat regularly; the freedom of "stardom" had become a financial burden he could no longer afford. While an occasional leading role came his way, he concentrated mainly on secondary parts, as the market for westerns continued to shrink throughout the rest of the twenties. But when the silents gave way to talkies, the double feature came into its own and created a demand for program films. Filling this demand became the province of the independent producer, who came back to the screen in a big way with the "B" western.

Big Boy Williams took another brief fling at stardom in an expanding market in the thirties (*Big Boy Rides Again, Danger Trails, Law of The .45's*) before settling into the comfortable roles he fitted so well—the dull-witted comic relief for the hero or the rough, tough heavy. Western fans of the forties and fifties invariably recognized his name on the opening credits and settled back into their seats to enjoy a superb performance by the veteran character actor who swiped scenes with the ease of a professional thief, not realizing that his consummate portrayals were the result of more years of experience than he cared to count. Death put an end to it all June 6, 1962, but thanks to television, those who appreciate good acting can occasionally catch Guinn Williams on the late show, a performance usually worth staying up to enjoy once more.

Jay Wilsey

(BUFFALO BILL JR.)

The second of Lester F. Scott's starring trio in the twenties, Jay Wilsey came to the screen from the rodeo circuits in 1922. A Hillsdale, Wyoming boy, Wilsey had made a name for himself as a cowboy with various Wild West shows and touring rodeos. Jay's picture debut came with stunt roles and bit parts under his own name; it was Scott who chose his stage name when he signed Wilsey to a contract in 1924. With less than two years experience in front of a camera, Jay Wilsey suddenly found himself on the threshold of stardom.

Placed in the single unit with Buddy Roosevelt, and later Wally Wales, Jay's pictures shared the production talents of Richard Thorpe and Betty Burbridge as several westerns were filmed by Ray Ries on an overlapping basis. Each of the Action Pictures westerns required about four to five days to shoot and another two days to cut and title. There was little time for rehearsals and less for retakes. When the crew had finished shooting a scene and were waiting for the next setup, they were busy studying the upcoming script, provided it was ready for them. More often than not, they worked with a one- or two-day lead on the story, and looking back now, Thorpe's work with his stars (and Miss Burbridge's ability to write faster than he could shoot) seems even more miraculous than it was at the time.

Made at a cost of between $10,000 and $15,000, the Action Pictures were quickie westerns in the truest sense of the word, yet they were well enough done in comparison to other independent westerns to capture the imagination of countless small boys *and* the respect of reviewers. Buffalo Bill Jr. made his first appearance on the screen in August 1924 with *Rarin' To Go* and Wilsey came off quite well in his first starring role. Although it was a trade paper, *The Motion Picture News* had adopted a hard line toward

Jay Wilsey.

the wares of independent producers in 1923–24, and while a weak Paramount picture might escape its wrath, a bad independent was unmercifully panned—or worse yet, it was passed by unnoticed. Thus, when *The News* commented on Jay's talent in the saddle and predicted popularity in a few short months, it was a glowing tribute to the ex-bronc buster, his writer and director.

Fast and Fearless followed, with a youthful Jean Arthur (in the days before her brunette tresses became blonde) as Wilsey's feminine lead and then *Hard-Hitting Hamilton*. Jay's easy manner on-camera, his lack of grandstand heroics and pre-sold name quickly

"There's no justice, old fellow." But Buffalo Bill Jr. always got his man and won the girl too.

gained him a following of fans anxious to share his light-hearted and sometimes off-beat adventures. Whether posing as a girl rancher's long-lost brother to help her fend off land grabbers (*The Interferin' Gent*), or helping a poor family regain its rightful possessions (*Pals in Peril*), Wilsey's early scripts were well above average in concept and treatment. *The Ballyhoo Buster* exemplified the unusual often found in Jay's films. Unable to face Peggy Shaw after having been fleeced out of the savings for their honeymoon, Buffalo Bill left town on a fast freight and joined a traveling medicine show where he recouped his loss. Itching to return to the scene of his disaster, Bill knew that the show's itinerary would eventually take him back, and meeting his malefactors he wrapped up the story with a rousing brawl before marrying the girl.

Another example of the unusual plot lines that lifted so many of the Action Pictures above the level of their competitors, *Rawhide* cast Buffalo Bill Jr. as a much-misunderstood hero; a gambler had accused him of committing a murder that never took place, the

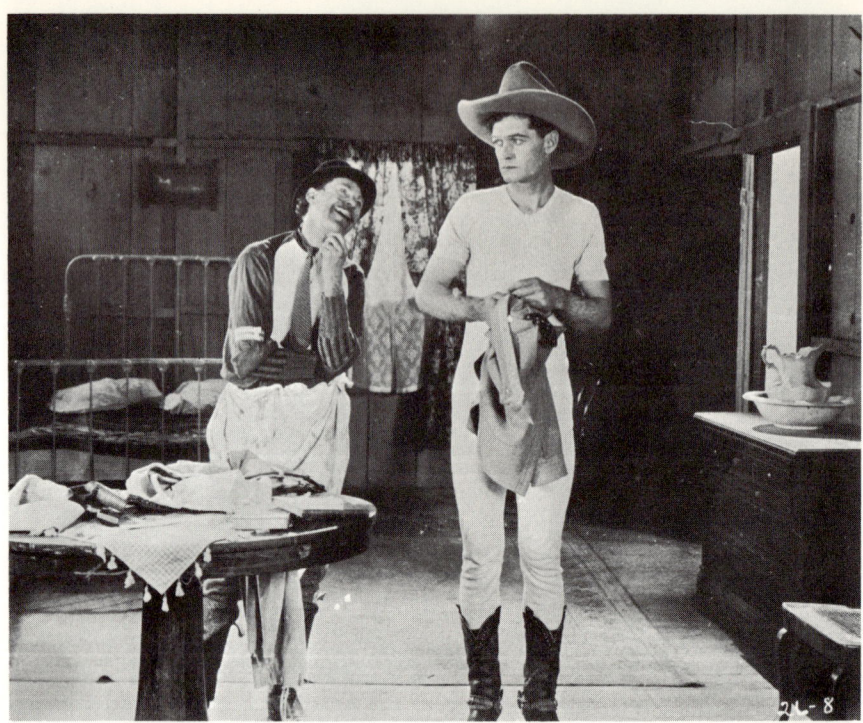

Harry Todd, whose career dated back to the western comedies of Alkali Ike at Essanay, carved a new niche for himself as comic support to Jay in the Buffalo Bill Jr. westerns.

Jay and Robert Walker.

Betty Baker, Jay Wilsey and a box of crackerjacks—what better way to spend a Sunday afternoon?

Roarin' Broncs, *one of the Buffalo Bill Jr. westerns.*

After smashing the villain's hideout with a tractor, Buffalo Bill Jr. and Harry Todd round up the outlaws.

presumed dead man's brother sought revenge and Molly Malone believed Bill guilty of a swindle that had resulted in the death of her father and sister. Although menaced by Al Taylor, Joe Rickson and Charles Whittaker, Bill managed to pull the tangled threads apart and solve the mystery. The film's major weakness rested in Miss Malone's attempt to portray a girl pretending blindness, a feat that failed badly and marred an otherwise excellent program western.

But originality on a monthly basis cannot continue forever (especially when it had to be sufficient to take care of two other series) and by mid-1927, the Buffalo Bill Jr. westerns had returned to the tried-and-true formula—fans of all three cowpokes soon noticed a marked similarity between a current Buffalo Bill Jr. picture and an earlier Wally Wales or Buddy Roosevelt oater, in content if not in treatment. The surprising thing is how long Betty Burbridge and Frank L. Inghram (Richard Thorpe) were able to keep it up.

By the close of 1928, Pathé had brought an end to the Buffalo Bill Jr. series, just as it had a year earlier with Buddy Roosevelt;

It was a crooked poker game, but Buffalo Bill Jr. didn't know it. Losing the money he had saved to marry Peggy Shaw, our hero had no choice but to leave town. Before The Ballyhoo Buster *was over, the score would be evened.*

but Wilsey's reputation was sufficiently well established to allow him the luxury of dropping the stage name and moving to Universal, where he starred with Louise Lorraine and Newton House in *A Final Reckoning*. Portraying an Australian law enforcement officer determined to foil a plot against Miss Lorraine and her brother, Jay endured burning buildings, wagons careening over cliffs and the deadly whip of his adversary (Ed Cobb) as he fought the chapter play through to its successful conclusion.

Immediately after finishing *A Final Reckoning*, Wilsey was cast as the lead in *Pirate of Panama* with former Sennett comedienne Natalie Kingston. If you can imagine a western pirate story, you've pegged this one. But like their western counterparts, serials were suffering from overexposure and a shrinking market; the onslaught of sound reduced production to a mere trickle. Trapped between a lack of work and the loss of what he had saved in the stock market crash of 1929, Jay Wilsey's career ran out of steam.

Jay went to Universal when Action Pictures closed its doors.

Following the pattern so well established by many of the silent sagebrush heroes, Jay had a few starring roles of obscure independents in the early thirties, then supporting roles which became bit parts. While his voice was quite satisfactory for talkies, Wilsey was in a surplus labor market—western leading men whose stardom had been circumscribed. In Jay's case, Lester Scott's ego had been partly responsible, the stage name, the small amount of publicity, a determination not to let his "stars" become the victims of swelled heads and ask for more money, and a firm conviction that *Lester F. Scott Jr. Presents* . . . . should make a greater impression on exhibitors and fans than *Buffalo Bill Jr. in* . . . .

Wilsey, a long-time yachting fan and hobbyist who built his own boats, left the screen to become the captain of a freighter plying the West Coast to South America and so disappeared into that mysterious Sargasso Sea of one-time screen idols whom circumstances and their own feet of clay had made vulnerable to the fickle whims of producers and the public. But his days of glory as Buffalo Bill Jr. still live on in countless thousands of fading memories belonging to the small boys, now grown to maturity, who cheered and clapped every Saturday afternoon.

★★★

And Others

We've come to the end of a long trail; one which carried us across the Pecos and over the Rockies, along the Santa Fé and Oregon Trails, through desert sandstorms and Yukon blizzards, from grassy plain to the land of the tall timber. We've chased rustlers, outlaws and fugitives; saved ranches, mining claims and the fur trade; fought Indians, Mexicans and outlaws, standing firm beside the Cavalry and Texas Rangers in their most glorious adventures. We've scouted with Kit Carson and built iron webs across the open plains. We helped Daniel Boone to open the West in the late 1700s and settled it with Jim Bridger and the other western scouts a century later, fighting every step of the way to make it safe for those who followed us.

The blazing sun has beat upon us; we've been drenched by raging storms and frozen by the bitter Arctic winters, and yet we have made it, almost to the finale. Oh, we had help along the way in our 26-year journey, much more than we've accounted for in the previous pages. There were many other heroes of the sagebrush who played a role in our journey than we have considered and although their importance may be questionable to some, no adventure of the magnitude such as the one we've just taken can really be finished until we've met some of them. The following pages contain a few of those personalities who played but a minor role in the celluloid battle for the old West, yet their names linger in the roll call of our memory like old friends, and here we pay our homage.

Fred Church and Eileen Sedgwick. Church began his western portrayals at Essanay before World War I and reached his peak popularity around 1916 when this picture was taken on the set of The Temple of Terror. *In the late Twenties, he reappeared as "Montana Bill" in an independent series for William Pizor. Miss Sedgwick and her sister Josie were cast in countless western features, serials and shorts for Universal. Retired today and living near UCLA in Los Angeles, she prefers not to discuss her screen career.*

Philip Yale Drew (1) as Young Buffalo in The Hobo of Pizen City. *This series of well-received westerns was produced by the Graphilm Corporation for Pathé release during 1920. Drew disappeared as rapidly as he had appeared, but the memory of Young Buffalo is a vivid one with those fans who saw his films.*

Marie Walcamp's career was well underway when she left the screen to marry her leading man in The Dragon's Net, *a Universal serial of 1919. Marie's popularity as a western and serial queen at Universal during World War I was unchallenged until her premature retirement. A return to the screen in the mid-twenties failed to regain her fans and she was seen mainly in independent westerns at that time. Marie is best remembered today for her serials and the* Tempest Cody *short subjects.*

J. P. McGowan (r) in The Hills of Missing Men. *This prolific actor-director-writer was the husband of Helen Holmes and together they made many memorable action epics adventure fans relished. McGowan's work is unusual in that there was so much of it and the quality ranged from quite good to very bad. He certainly let no moss grow under his feet in those days and worked well into the sound era. His early work as a screen hero was overshadowed by the later portrayals of villains for which fans of the thirties recall him best.*

James B. Warner died of tuberculosis in 1924 at the age of 29, shortly after completing his second starring series. Warner had supported Pete Morrison in 1921–22 and then made 18 western short subjects for Cliff Elfelt (Flaming Hearts, Crimson Gold, Danger) before joining Sunset Productions for The Lone Fighter, Behind Two Guns, Treasure Canyon, etc. His starring career encompassed only 16 feature films, and as little promotional work was done for them, hardly any stills or lobby cards remain in existence—a situation similar to the silent films of Guinn "Big Boy" Williams.

George Kesterson (clenched fist) was presented to fans in the mid-twentiés by Denver Dixon as Art Mix. Only a few of these films were made before an injunction stopped the use of the name Mix. Dixon however seemed to regard it as his own personal property and several other actors appeared on the screen as either Art Mix or Bill Mix. Kesterson was seen mainly in supporting roles until well into the thirties and made a much better villain than hero.

Bill Patton was noted mainly for his Universal comic melodramas which emphasized comedy quite heavily. Patton's starring career was an on-off affair, liberally sprinkled with supporting roles.

Newton House and Louise Lorraine in Universal's 1929 serial, A Final Reckoning. *House graduated to starring roles in 1927 with the two-reel* Champion Boy Rider *series at Universal and offered Buzz Barton the only competition the little redhead met up with in the closing days of the silent western.*

Bob Reeves began his screen career with Universal around World War I. He starred in Universal's 1920 serial, The Great Radium Mystery, *but his career stalled badly in the twenties. Reeves's western feature roles were mainly for Rayart in 1925–27; his western short subjects were for Universal. Bob made little impression on western fans.*

Fred Gilman was another juvenile who came to the fore just as the silent period was ending. A talented rider and fighter, he was the star of Universal's Texas Ranger *series in 1927–28.*

Hero of the "Stunt Cowboy" series for Universal in 1927–28, Bob Curwood was supposedly related to the famous writer James Oliver Curwood. Bob's starring career came to an embarrassing close in 1929 when he couldn't find work in westerns and tried without success to form his own company.

Kermit Maynard, older brother of Ken, appeared in a Trem Carr series for Rayart in 1925, billed as "Tex" Maynard. This scene is from "A Prince of The Plains". Kermit's career in the silents never left the ground, even though he changed his name to Tex Austin in the late twenties. Independent westerns of the thirties would feature this daredevil stuntman prominently but although a better actor Kermit failed to achieve the same fame as his younger brother.

Groomed for stardom by Leo Maloney, Don Coleman was cast in supporting roles in many of the Maloney westerns with Leo finally giving him leading roles in 1928–29; but Coleman's starring career ended with Maloney's death. This scene from Black Aces, a Pathé release of 1928, contains J. P. McGowan, Coleman, Noble Johnson and Ben Corbett. Corbett would make an interesting series of three-reelers with Jack Perrin in the thirties.

Rex Bell and Ruth Mix. Bell was born George Belden in Chicago and came to the screen in the late twenties. Popular for a time, he bought a ranch in Nevada in 1930 and gradually retired from the screen after marrying Clara Bow to devote himself to ranching and politics. His great achievement came in 1954 when he was elected Lieutenant-Governor of Nevada. Rex died July 4, 1962. Ruth Mix was the daughter of Tom and appeared in a series of independent westerns against her father's wishes. Ruth failed to make any lasting impression on fans and is all but forgotten today.

Coming to the screen after World War I as C. Edward Hatton, this hero won greater fame in the twenties as Dick Hatton, working for Arrow, FBO, Rayart and Pathé.

And finally, Lee Meehan, whose villainy graced so many westerns of the twenties that he must have had three doubles, lends a helping hand.

920
L
Lahue
Winners of the West: the sage-
   brush heroes of the silent screen